A
GOURMET'S
GUIDE TO

HERBS
&
SPICES

A
GOURMET'S
GUIDE TO

HERBS
&
SPICES

MARY TREWBY

Photographed by
DAVID JOHNSON

HPBooks
a division of
PRICE STERN SLOAN
Los Angeles

ANOTHER BEST SELLING VOLUME FROM HPBOOKS

HPBooks
A division of Price Stern Sloan, Inc.
360 North La Cienega Boulevard
Los Angeles, California 90048
9 8 7 6 5 4 3 2 1

This book was created by Merehurst Limited
Ferry House, 51/57 Lacy Road, London SW15 1PR

Commissioned and Directed by Merehurst Limited.
Photography: David Johnson
Food Stylist: Kay McGlone
Home Economist: Lyn Rutherford
Designer: Peartree Design Associates
Color reproduction by Kentscan, England
Printed in Belgium by Proost International Book Production, Turnhout

Library of Congress Cataloging-in-Publication Data

Trewby, Mary.
    A gourmet's guide to herbs & spices / Mary Trewby ; photography by
David Johnson.
        p.   cm.
    Includes index.
    ISBN 0-89586-813-X
    1. Cookery (Herbs)   2. Herbs.   3. Spices   I. Title.
TX819.H4T74   1984
641.6'57—dc20
                                                                89-7463
                                                                CIP

Contents

Introduction

One of the most wonderful meals I've eaten was in Portugal, on a windswept cliff overlooking the Atlantic. It was late spring, one of those pale warm days that are so full of expectation. The food was simple and perfect—a soup laden with garlic, a piece of charcoal-grilled fish flavored with fresh cilantro. The taste of the cilantro was memorable, and typical of Portuguese cooking. If I'd been eating grilled fish in Italy, probably rosemary or thyme would have been used.

The flavors and the aromas of dishes depend very much on herbs and spices. And the choice of herbs and spices is determined by the place as well as the particular food. We associate chervil, tarragon and marjoram with France; cumin and the other curry spices with India; allspice with the West Indies; fresh ginger with Asia. And, of course, some spices and herbs are essential to a dish: no self-respecting Italian or Spanish cook would dream of making a risotto or paella without saffron, for instance. Tradition plays an important role in the kitchen.

The traditions are based on centuries of wise experiment, and on what is fashionable. This is particularly true when it comes to herbs. Until very recently, spices were expensive, highly prized commodities and in some cases worth more than their weight in gold. Products with such economic importance rarely are allowed to disappear from the market place. But herbs have never cost much, and the dividing line between a "weed" and an herb is a fine one. Dandelion, lovage and salad burnet, for example, were much used up until the end of the last century, then their culinary importance was all but forgotten, which is a pity, as many of the more unusual herbs are excellent included in salads.

Herbs are often added as a garnish. Flowers used to be, and once more it's time to strew them in your salads and on desserts. Good food should taste wonderful and look beautiful.

Basil

Lettuce-leaf basil

One of the truly great culinary herbs, basil *(Ocimum basicicum)* is an essential ingredient for all cooking enthusiasts. The plant probably originated in India although it is little used there. It is in the Middle East and the Mediterranean countries that basil is greatly appreciated, undoubtedly because it thrives in warm climates and cannot stand frost. It is an annual plant, with light green ovate leaves.

There are over forty types of basil from which to choose. Sweet or common basil—the main culinary variety—boasts the finest flavor, with the larger leaved lettuce-leaf basil a close second. The flavors of the other popular types—purple-leaved variety and the low-growing bush or dwarf basil—are inferior; they are grown more for their looks. Other varieties include curly or Italian basil and lemon basil. The plant known as wild or hedge basil is related to calamint, not basil, and is quite different in taste.

The young leaves are the sweetest, so the plants should be sown regularly and used when only six to nine inches high. Basil is quite successful grown in window-boxes or sunny kitchens—its perfume seems to fill the home with the aroma of summer.

The flavor of fresh basil is sweet, fragrant and spicy; it seems stronger and fresher in the middle of a hot summer, somehow intensified by the heat. It is one herb that cannot be dried successfully—the taste is quite unlike that of the fresh herb. It can be quick frozen, however, although it loses its color unless blanched first, or preserved in a good quality olive oil. It also makes a fine herb vinegar (see page 66).

The best basil is reputed to grow around the Italian city of Genoa on the shores of the Mediterranean. This is the home of *pesto*, the famous basil sauce served with pasta. It is made by pounding the fresh herb with garlic, pine nuts and grated Parmesan cheese. A similar preparation, but often without the pine nuts, is used to flavor soups on the nearby Provençal coast.

Basil features prominently in the cuisine of Italy, southern France, Spain, Greece, North Africa and the Middle East. The sweetness and fresh taste lends itself especially to egg dishes, and it is frequently used in omelettes and scrambled eggs. It is excellent with fish, notably lobsters and red mullet, Mediterranean vegetables, such as eggplant, zucchini and bell peppers and has a particular affinity with tomatoes. Basil is the common flavoring in the tomato salads and sauces of Italy and the south of France. It is best added to hot dishes just before serving, otherwise it tends to lose its flavor. The leaves should be torn rather than chopped, again to preserve their flavor.

Purple-leaf basil

Dwarf basil

Italian basil

Common basil

Bay Leaves

The bay tree *(Laurus nobilis)*, native to the Mediterranean, is a small, shrubby evergreen with wonderful aromatic leaves. It is often grown as an ornamental tree, although it can reach up to 65 feet.

The bay tree's dark green ovate leaves are indispensable in cooking, used fresh or dried. As they are dried, the leaves turn a pale greyish-green and mellow, losing the bitterness characteristic of the fresh leaves. However, dried bay leaves should not be kept too long, as they tend to lose their flavor.

Bay leaves are used extensively throughout the world to flavor stews, soups, stocks and marinades, with meat and fish dishes, and in bouquet garnis (see page 36). They are particularly associated with French and Mediterranean cooking. They are also excellent in rice puddings, essential in the great spicy *Cajun gumbo* fish stews, and often used to flavor drinks and puddings.

The ancient Romans used the black berries of the bay, which resemble olives, pounded with other fragrant seeds and herbs, as a sauce.

Chives

Chives *(Allium schoenoprasum)* grow in clumps, have thin, cylindrical grass-like leaves, which are bright green, and produce purple pompom flowers. They are easy to grow in pots or in the garden, and are popular in decorative borders.

Chives are a member of the onion family and their flavor is similar but more delicate. They are used chopped as a garnish in sauces and soups and on salads and vegetables. They go particularly well with eggs. Chives are also a classic component of fines herbes (see page 36).

Chives are best kept in a sealed plastic bag in the refrigerator or freezer. But, as they can be grown so easily, it is possible to have fresh chives on hand most of the year.

Cilantro/Coriander

Coriander *(Coriandrum sativum)* is a slender annual which grows up to 2 feet high. It is easy to grow and an extremely useful and distinctive culinary addition.

As well as being one of the most ancient herbs known, coriander is one of the most widely used.

The leaves look slightly similar to flat-leaved parsley, but coriander is recognizable by its lighter green color and distinctive smell. The plant is also harvested for its seed, used as a spice (see page 51).

Coriander leaves taste quite different from the seeds. The leaves are sharp and aromatic with a freshness quite unlike any other herb. They are used to flavor vegetable dishes, with fish and meat, and as a garnish.

Cilantro (Fresh coriander)

Chives

Dill

Dill *(Anethum graveolens)* is grown for its fine feathery leaves—dill weed—and seeds (see page 51). A native of southern Europe, it is now found all over the world. An annual or biennial, the plant grows to about 3 feet. It is easy to grow, but often difficult to find on sale.

Dill was well known to the ancient world: there is evidence that the Egyptians used it medicinally. Its name comes from the Norse word *dilla*, meaning "to lull," a reference to the dill water from its seeds which is still given to babies as a mild sedative.

The flavor of the leaves has been variously described as being like fennel or parsley, although it is sweeter and more aromatic than either. The subtleness of dill makes it a perfect partner for fish.

The leaves are not as widely used as they deserve to be, except by the Scandinavians, Germans, and central and eastern Europeans. Dill is used in the famous Swedish pickled raw salmon dish, Gravlax, and mainly with vegetables and fish, notably salmon. It goes well with yogurt, thick sour cream and eggs, and makes an excellent wine vinegar.

Marjoram

Marjoram is a sweet-scented herb characteristic of the Mediterranean. It is used extensively in the meat and poultry dishes, stuffings, sausages, garlic-flavored dishes and pizzas commonly eaten in the south of France and Italy, and with the grilled meats of Greece.

There are, in fact three different marjorams. Sweet or knotted marjoram *(Origanum majorana)*, the most delicate flavored, prefers a hot sun and is the one used in French cooking. It has a great affinity with thyme, and the two herbs are often substituted for one another or mixed together. When used fresh, it is best added towards the end of cooking time, otherwise it tends to lose its flavor; it also makes an excellent aromatic addition to summer salads. Sweet marjoram is delicious fresh but, like all the marjorams, seems to become more aromatic when dried.

Pot marjoram *(O. onites)* is also of Mediterranean origin, but is much hardier and therefore the type usually grown in colder climates. Its flavor is stronger and not as sweet as sweet marjoram. Pot marjoram is important in the cooking of Greece, where it grows wild.

The third marjoram is the herb which is known as oregano *(O. vulgare)*. It has a pungent flavor, and is the strongest of the three. It is important in Italy, especially in the south where it adds its distinctive flavor to the classic pizza of Naples. The Italians add oregano to all kinds of meat, fish and vegetable dishes, generally using it in its dried form. Golden marjoram *(O. vulgare aureum)* is an attractive variety of oregano, which has golden leaves.

Sweet marjoram

Golden marjoram

Pot marjoram

Golden-tipped marjoram

Oregano

Mint

There are a vast number of mints, many of them hybrids. They all share the same cool, refreshing, aromatic taste of menthol: the quantity of menthol the mint contains varies, which affects the flavor. There are three mints commonly cultivated and used for culinary purposes: spearmint, apple mint and peppermint.

Spearmint *(Mentha viridis or M. spicata)* is the best known and most widely used of the culinary mints. It has long pointed leaves and an upright stem. It is a Mediterranean native, much used by the ancient Romans.

Apple or Bowles mint *(M. rotundifolia),* one of the best of all mints, is a large round-leafed variety which combines the taste of mint with that of apples. It is sweeter and mellower than most of the other mints.

Peppermint *(M. piperita),* with its deep red stem and red-blushed long leaves, is a hybrid of spearmint and water mint. It contains the most menthol, making it the strongest mint. Peppermint leaves are rarely used in food; they are generally made into oil of peppermint. This is used to flavor liqueurs, peppermint candies and chocolates.

Water mint *(M. aquatica)* is one of the less important mints. It grows prolifically in very wet conditions and is rather rank tasting.

The fragrant eau de Cologne mint *(M. citrata)* has a delicate flavor variously described: its other common

names—orange mint, lavender mint and bergamot mint—reflect difference of opinion about its flavor.

Pennyroyal *(M. pulegium)* is another common mint, mainly dried and used for teas. It is said to repel mosquitoes and fleas, and is used as a contraceptive in China.

Other mints cultivated for the herb garden include Pineapple mint, which has variegated green and white leaves, and Corsican mint *(M. requienii).* Mints are widely used in India, the Levant, the Middle East and North Africa; quite frequently in Spain and Italy; but hardly at all by the French, who find them a little vulgar. In Britain, of course, the use of mint with lamb is a well-known tradition. Spearmint and the famous vinegar-based mint sauce were introduced by the Romans.

As well as lamb, mint is used with strong-flavored meats such as mutton and duck. It has a distinctive summer taste and goes particularly well with the vegetables that are identified with that season such as tomatoes, cucumbers, new potatoes, eggplants and zucchini. Mint is also a refreshing addition to many fruit dishes—for instance, those made with the berry fruits—and is an indispensable ingredient in the true mint julep cocktail. It is also used in fruit salads, punches and iced teas, while the dried herb is commonly made into teas (see page 70).

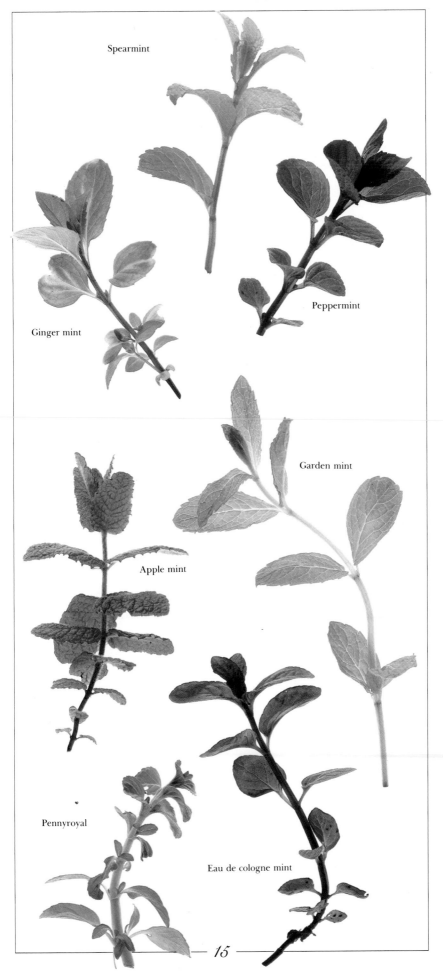

Spearmint

Ginger mint

Peppermint

Garden mint

Apple mint

Pennyroyal

Eau de cologne mint

Parsley

Parsley *(Petroselinum crispum)* is probably the most popular and versatile herb available. The two main kinds of parsley are the curly-leaved varieties, grown extensively in England, America, Australia and New Zealand, and the flat-leaved types, often called Hamburg or continental parsley.

Parsley is a biennial that grows very well in window boxes and pots. The leaves of the curled variety are divided into segments, the edges of which are tightly curled. Flat-leaved parsley can be confused with fool's parsley, which is poisonous.

The origins of the parsley plant are much disputed: some say it is a native of Sardinia, others claim its origin lies in the eastern Mediterranean. One thing is certain: parsley is indispensable in the kitchen and it is essential to have a constant supply on hand to enhance your cooking.

Parsley helps to bring out the flavor of other herbs and is therefore always included in bouquet garni and in fines herbes mixture (see page 36).

Parsley is used with all types of fish, shellfish, meat, poultry and game and is often sprinkled on vegetable dishes. It is a common ingredient in sauces and stuffings; parsley sauce is a traditional accompaniment for fish.

It is often put into a dish at the beginning of cooking and then more added, finely chopped, as a garnish at the end. A light parsley soup is delicious in summer and whole stalks of the herb are sometimes fried and served as a vegetable. Of all garnishes, parsley is the one most commonly used.

Rich in vitamins and certain trace elements, such as iron and calcium, the herb's medicinal uses are many: it was once widely used for liver and kidney complaints. There are numerous legends concerning parsley: the Romans used it to counteract the effects of alcohol and to sweeten the breath, while the Greeks regarded parsley as a symbol of death.

Rosemary

Rosemary *(Rosmarinus officinalis)* is a strong flavored herb. In many places this shrub is cultivated for its sweet scent and attractive appearance, rather than for culinary purposes. The rosemary bush has spiky evergreen leaves and produces small flowers. A dwarf variety of rosemary *(R. lavendulaceus)* is available.

The word rosemary means "dews of the sea" for the plant grows wild all around the Mediterranean coast. It thrives in sunny positions and is often used as an edging plant.

It is the Italians who make the best use of rosemary as a herb, flavoring roasted meats and poultry with it, using it in vegetable dishes, sprinkling it on breads and burning rosemary branches under grilled fish and meats to impart flavor.

It is used to a lesser extent in English, Spanish and French cooking, although in bygone days it was much more valued: rosemary was once used to flavor breads and wine and the pale blue flowers were sometimes candied and eaten as a confection.

Rosemary leaves were also infused to make hair rinses and toilet waters and these natural products are once again seeing a revival. The essential oil of rosemary is used in perfumery.

Because they are a little leathery, rosemary leaves must be chopped very finely for culinary use. Or, whole sprigs used in stews and soups or laid on meat before grilling or roasting and removed before serving.

Rosemary sprigs are also used to make an excellent flavored vinegar and oil (see page 66).

Curly-leaf parsley

Flat-leaf parsley

Rosemary

Dwarf rosemary

Sage

There are several different types of sage—for example, purple, golden and variegated leaf varieties; pineapple and lavender flavored ones. The less common types include pink and white flowering varieties.

The most common sage used in cooking is garden sage *(Salvia officinalis)* which has purple flowers and grey leaves. Narrow-leaved, blue-flowering sage is also excellent for culinary purposes.

Sage is another herb appreciated more by the Italians than most others, although northern Europeans do make use of it. It has a powerful flavor, pungent and aromatic with a slight camphor taste.

The Italians use sage in meat dishes, most notably with calf liver and veal, but also simply chopped and used with butter as a sauce for pasta—in fact, sage is used a great deal in pasta sauces. The Germans even flavor eels with sage. In the Mediterranean countries, sage leaves are often threaded onto skewers with cubes of meat and vegetables. It is an ingredient in certain cheeses and sausages and its use mixed with onions as a stuffing for pork and poultry is well-known.

Sage dries well, although it takes longer than most herbs, and it is also suitable for quick freezing.

Tarragon

Strongly identified as a French herb, the spiky leaved tarragon is little used by anyone else. Nevertheless, it is one of the great culinary herbs with a sophistication and refinement that is quite unique.

There are two types of tarragon: French tarragon *(Artemesia dracunculus)*, the finer flavored variety, and Russian tarragon *(A. dracunculoides)*, which has larger, paler leaves. The herb was introduced to Europe by the Moors. A bush perennial, it is quite difficult to grow from seed—propagating from rooted shoots is more successful. Tarragon requires a well-drained sunny position and does well in pots and window boxes.

Tarragon is used to flavor egg dishes and omelettes and it is one of the four ingredients in fines herbes (see page 36). It goes particulary well with chicken: *poulet à l'estragon* is a famous French dish. Tarragon is used with roasted meats and fish, and is essential in sauce béarnaise, sauce tartare and in many cream sauces. The leaves are also often added to salads and vegetable dishes.

Tarragon vinegar, made by steeping stems of tarragon leaves in wine vinegar, gives an excellent flavor to mayonnaise and vinaigrettes and is much used in prepared mustards.

The herb can be quick frozen, but drying distorts its flavor too much and is not recommended.

French
tarragon

Golden sage

Pineapple sage

Variegated-leaf sage

Purple-leaf sage

Thyme

Garden thyme

Garden thyme *(Thymus vulgaris)* is a powerfully aromatic herb with a strong, slightly bitter flavor which is due to the volatile oil thymol. It is a low evergreen with tiny leaves and blue flowers—one of over a hundred varieties of thyme and the kind most favored for cooking. The other favorite culinary thyme is Lemon thyme *(T. citriodorus);* this has a citrus taste and is often used where a more subtle flavor is required. There are also orange and caraway flavored thymes and many decorative varieties, including silver thyme and golden-edged thyme.

Thyme is one of the most important culinary herbs of Europe and was recognized as such by the ancient Greeks. Today it is widely used in all the Mediterranean countries and is indispensable in the French kitchen. It is easy to grow, from seed or cuttings, and thrives in the garden or in window-boxes. It also dries extremely well. Every serious cook should have a choice of several varieties at hand.

An essential herb in bouquet garni (see page 36), thyme is also used to flavor stocks, stuffings and soup. It goes well with fish and vegetables such as potatoes, beans and peppers, and is especially good in lamb, beef, poultry and game dishes cooked slowly with wine and garlic. It is excellent with grilled meat and fish and is often added to herb butters. Olives are sometimes flavored with sprigs of thyme. Lemon thyme can be used in preference to stronger garden thyme with fish and in egg dishes. It also adds an aromatic zest to fruit dishes.

Silver thyme

Wooley thyme

Lemon thyme

Golden-tipped thyme

Golden thyme

E. B. Anderson thyme

Angelica

Angelica *(Angelica archangelica)* is a giant member of the parsley family, growing to over 6 feet high with thick, hollow stems, large bright green leaves, white flowers and a strong sweet scent. It is a biennial, native to northern Europe, Russia, Iceland and Greenland, thriving in a cool damp climate.

According to tradition, the herb got its angelic connections from an archangel who recommended its use at the time of the plague. It has been widely used through the ages for its medicinal qualities, particularly as a cure for indigestion.

The best known use of angelica is in its candied form, when the young green stems are served as confections and used as an attractive decoration for cakes and sweet dishes. But every part of the plant can be used.

The sweet pungent leaves are added to tart fruit dishes and jams, herb mixtures and fish dishes or they too can be candied. The young shoots are blanched and used in salads. The leaves are sometimes dried and used as a tisane (see page 70). In northern Europe and some parts of Italy, the stems are treated as a vegetable in a similar manner to asparagus.

The taste of angelica slightly resembles that of juniper and the essential oils made from its seeds, leaves and roots are used with juniper to flavor gin, vermouths and liqueurs such as Anisette and Chartreuse.

Borage

Bergamot

Bergamot

A native of North America, bergamot *(Monarda didyma)* has light green ovate leaves, shaggy red flowerheads and an orange scent. Another variety, wild bergamot *(M. fistulosa)*, smells of lemons. Bergamot likes a moist rich soil and some sun.

Its best known use is as a tisane (see page 70). During the Boston Tea Party of 1773, the settlers drank tea made from bergamot leaves rather than that imported from Britain.

The young leaves are used in salads and also go well with pork. Bergamot flowers can be added to salads and make a pretty decoration for desserts and iced drinks.

Borage

Borage *(Borago officinalis)* is an annual and a common wild flower in Europe and America. It grows to about 3 feet.

The five-pointed sky-blue flower, with its distinctive black center, is the most obvious reason for growing this plant. But the grey-green leaves, which taste remarkably like cucumber, have a variety of uses; they can be cooked in similar ways to spinach, added to pickles and used as a gar-nish. Borage leaves can also be added to salads and iced drinks, such as Pimms or wine cups, but they are covered with fine hairs and must be chopped finely.

The flowers are sometimes candied, but their main use is to decorate drinks, desserts and salads. In medieval times, they were believed to be a cure for melancholy.

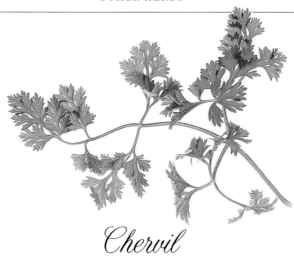

Chervil

Chervil *(Anthriscus cerefolium)* is strangely neglected outside France, even though it is easily grown. A biennial, the plant likes moist semishady conditions and grows to about 18 inches high. The pale green lacy leaves, which should be picked off constantly, have a delicate, slightly sweet taste a little like fennel; both smooth-leaved and curly varieties are available.

A classic French herb, chervil is one of the four fines herbes (see page 36) for an omelette and is an essential ingredient in sauce ravigote (see page 88). It can be used in salads, sauces and soups—much like parsley—but is more subtle and should be added to dishes at the very last moment and in quantity. It combines well with both saffron and tarragon and is also used to flavor wine vinegar (see page 70).

Chervil is always best used fresh.

Clary

A little-used herb outside southern Europe these days, clary *(Salvia sclarea)* was more widely grown until the 18th century. It was used as an eye wash and made into wine.

Clary is an interesting salad green with large heart-shaped leaves and a slightly bitter taste. Because they are hairy, the leaves should be chopped before using raw in salads. The whole leaves are excellent dipped in batter and fried.

Comfrey

Comfrey *(Symphytum officinale)* is a grey-green perennial with long hairy leaves. Both the leaves and stalks are used in cooking: the young leaves are cooked in much the same way as spinach or chopped finely and eaten raw in salads. The stalks should be trimmed and blanched and served as asparagus is served.

Comfrey has many medicinal uses, including a cough remedy brewed from its roots and leaves.

Curry Leaf

The curry plant *(Chalcas koenigii)* is a native of Southeast Asia. It is grown principally in southern India for its leaf, which is an essential ingredient—and the predominant aroma and flavor—in Madras curry powder. Many southern Indian dishes are flavored with the leaves and it is popular in Southeast Asia and Africa.

Curry leaves are shaped rather like bay leaves. In India they are generally used fresh. Dried curry leaves are usually available from shops specializing in Indian and Chinese food; sometimes fresh leaves are stocked too. These can be dried in the oven or quick frozen.

Clary

Comfrey

Curry leaf

Fennel

The ancient Romans were very fond of fennel in all its forms—the feathery herb, the aromatic seed and the bulbous vegetable—and made great use of it, introducing it to the far reaches of their empire. To the Romans fennel was a symbol of flattery and it was one of the nine sacred herbs of the Anglo-Saxons.

Fennel is a native of southern Europe. The plant used as a herb looks rather similar to dill with fine bright green leaves and yellow flower-heads, but grows to some 6 feet. There are two main types: Sweet or Roman fennel *(Foeniculum vulgare)* tastes strongly of anise, while there is little or no trace of this in the slightly bitter wild fennel, the type which is grown in central and eastern Europe.

The seeds harvested from the herb or the bulbous vegetable Florence fennel *(F. vulgare dulce)* are used as a spice (see page 52). The leaves of Florence fennel can be used in the same way as those of sweet fennel, but they have less flavor.

The Italians of today are just as enthusiastic as their ancestors about fennel: they use the leaves with pork and veal, in soups and salads and, of course, with fish. For centuries fennel has been used all over Europe as a flavoring for fish, in accompanying sauces and stuffings or as a garnish. Sometimes a whole fish is grilled on a bed of dried fennel.

Lemon Balm

Lemon balm *(Melissa officinalis)* is a small evergreen of Mediterranean origin. The plant, which is easily grown, has oblong light green leaves which have the taste and smell of sweet lemon.

It is also known as *melissa,* the Greek word for bee (which is greatly attracted to the plant); *eau de melissa* is distilled from the herb.

Lemon balm is excellent chopped and used in salads, soups and egg dishes and is frequently used with fish. Fresh leaves can be floated on summer cocktails; dried, it can be made into a tea (see page 70).

Lemon Grass

A common ingredient in Southeast Asian cooking, lemon grass *(Cymbopogon citratus & C. flexuosus)* thrives in tropical climates. It has a bulbous base from which its long lemon-flavored leaves grow.

Lemon grass is available at oriental stores. It should be peeled and finely chopped before use and freezes well. If lemon grass is unavailable, lemon peel can usually be substituted.

The dried grass is also ground and sold as sereh powder: one teaspoon equals one lemon grass stalk.

Lovage

With its distinctive savory taste somewhat similar to celery, lovage *(Levisticum officinale)* is a useful garden herb, albeit widely neglected. It is a tall stout perennial, growing 6 to 7 feet and a native of southern Europe. It likes rich, moist soil and is easily grown from seed or propagated from the root.

In the past, lovage was widely used as a vegetable, treated in a similar way to celery. Like angelica, its young stems were candied and its seeds were used on cakes and breads. But fashions changed and lovage was all but forgotten.

Now it is only in Czechoslovakia and Italy where the whole lovage plant is used. Elsewhere, it is grown principally for its strong-tasting dark green leaves and young stalks which are finely chopped and added to stews, soups and salads, often as a substitute for celery. In fact, lovage is an interesting herb in its own right and deserves wider recognition.

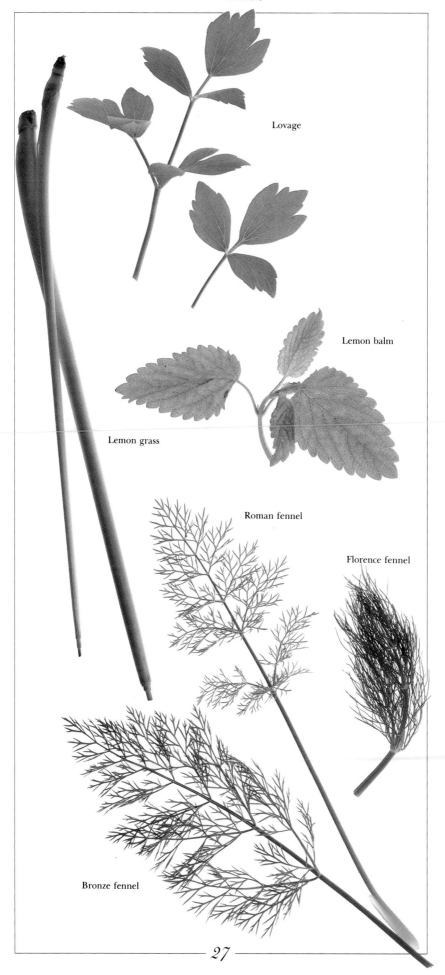

Lovage

Lemon balm

Lemon grass

Roman fennel

Florence fennel

Bronze fennel

Winter savory

Summer savory

Savory

There are two main culinary varieties. Summer savory *(Satureja hortensis)* is an annual, strongly aromatic with small narrow leaves. It thrives in sun and a fairly rich soil. Winter savory *(S. montana)* is a hardy perennial and has a tidier growing habit than the summer type. Both of these savories can be successfully dried.

Savory has a flavor a little like thyme, but is hot and peppery. In Europe it is commonly used with beans and peas; to flavor fish, particularly trout; with meats, and in sausages and stuffings. It is also an excellent addition to vegetable juices.

Sweet Cicely

The large, feathery leaves of the sweet cicely plant *(Myrrhis odorata)* are sweet-tasting with just a hint of anise.

The plant is a native of both northern Europe and America. A perennial, it likes partial shade and can be easily grown from seed, reaching a height of about 3 feet.

The leaves are used to sweeten puddings and fruit dishes, eaten raw in salads and cooked as a vegetable. The roots can also be eaten: grated raw as a salad, or boiled and served with butter. A tea made from the leaves is said to cure indigestion.

Tansy

A rather hot, bitter-tasting herb, tansy *(Chrysanthemum vulgare)* is a common wild plant, used as a herb until the 17th century but not much cultivated for kitchen use today. However, it can be used to flavor omelettes, custards, cakes, stuffings for rich meats and freshwater fish.

Tansy is one of the bitter herbs of the Jewish passover.

Sweet cicely

Tansy

Cress

Garden cress

The characteristic hot, peppery taste of watercress is shared by a number of plants that are called cresses and which all belong to the *Cruciferae* family: garden cress (also known as land cress, peppercress, peppergrass), American cress (variously called Belle Isle cress, land cress, mustard greens, scurvy grass, treacle mustard, treacle wormseed, upland cress, winter cress, wormseed and yellow rocket), Brazil cress and Indian cress.

The main use of these plants is as a salad green or garnish, as a pureed vegetable, or to flavor fish or a sauce. Watercress, in particular, makes a delicious soup. Cresses are an excellent source of vitamin C and iron.

Watercress

Most of the watercress *(Rorippa nasturtium-aquaticum)* available in stores and markets is cultivated; because of the danger of contamination, it is safer to eat than the wild watercress gathered from a stream. Watercress is bought by the bunch;

store in a cool place with its stems in water and use within two days.

Garden cress

Although garden cress *(Lepidium sativum)*, which is one half of "mustard and cress," is generally cropped at the seedling stage, it can be grown to a height of 12 to 18 inches, and is extremely useful as a salad vegetable. Cropped in its usual form, it is good used in sandwiches.

American Cress

American cress *(Barbarea verna)* is a much under-used variety. It is a hardy biennial, a native of Europe, and, if sown late in the summer, can provide salad greens right through until the spring. It has a stronger flavor than watercress, but this pepperiness is most attractive during the winter months. This cress is rarely on sale because it does not keep long once picked, so to be sure of a supply it is best grown from seed.

Watercress

Dandelion

The young leaves of the dandelion plant *(Taraxacum officinale)* are an interesting addition to spring salads. They have a slightly bitter, sharp taste and are sometimes blanched before use. Cook these like spinach.

The bright yellow dandelion flower is made into wine, and the roots, roasted and ground, are used to make a coffee. It is an extremely wholesome plant containing vitamins, proteins and mineral salts, and has been used for centuries as a healing plant.

Dandelion, of course, grows wild as a weed, although the French cultivate it and sell it in the markets. It is very easy to grow.

Lamb's Lettuce

Also known as corn salad, and *mâche* in France, lamb's lettuce *(Valerianella locusta)* is one of those valuable salad greens that is easy to grow and widely neglected, but once more regaining popularity. It is a low-growing hardy annual with long, bright green ovate leaves, which have a slightly astringent taste. The leaves are used when young, either raw in salads or cooked in the same ways as spinach.

Nettle

Despite its stinging ability, the nettle *(Urtica dioica)* is an interesting culinary herb, a perennial with valuable medicinal properties. It should be picked young in the spring, when the leaves are bright green. (Take care always to wear gloves.) The nettle has a sharp, slightly bitter taste.

Traditionally, nettles were used to flavor a potato-based soup or a broth, and they are also excellent made into a beer. Nettles are made into a wine too. They can also be cooked like spinach and eaten as a vegetable, or served with eggs.

Nettle

Lamb's lettuce

Rocket

Purslane

Purslane

The ovate leaves of purslane *(Portulaca oleracea)* are thick and fleshy and taste sharp and slightly nutty. Purslane is widely cultivated in the Middle East and India, where it is cooked and eaten as a vegetable or finely chopped and added as a herb to salads. In France, where it is kown as *pourpier*, the young leaves are made into a salad. The leaves can also be used to flavor soups and can be pickled.

Rocket

A strongly flavored salad green, rocket *(Eruca sativa)* is much used in Italy and the south of France; it is known as *arugula* or *rugula* in Italy. A native of the Mediterranean region, it is an easily grown annual which reaches a height of about 2 feet and produces long, bright green, lobed leaves.

One of the most interesting of salad greens, it is usually combined with other salad vegetables or used to flavor green herb sauces. It resembles the cress in its pungency.

Salad Burnet

Salad burnet *(Poterium sanguisorba)* was widely used throughout Europe in Elizabethan times and was taken to America by the Pilgrims. Its use declined, like so many other herbs, and now it is mainly in the Mediterranean countries, its region of origin.

This small perennial, which grows to about 12 inches is an excellent salad green, and finely chopped it is used in ravigote sauce and savory butters. The lacy leaves have a smell and taste rather like cucumber and, similarly, they are sometimes added to iced drinks.

Sorrel

Sorrel is a member of the dock family. There are two varieties commonly used in the kitchen, both of them native to Europe. French sorrel *(Rumes scutatus)* or round-leaved sorrel is the better one; it has a finer flavor and is less acid than the garden sorrel *(R. acetosa)*.

Sorrel leaves look like young spinach and, indeed, they are cooked in the same ways. They also taste similar, though sorrel has an acidity missing in spinach.

Sorrel is widely used in Europe and the Mediterranean. The French make sorrel soups and tarts, use it in sauces for fish, add it to omelettes and meat stews, and serve the young leaves as a vegetable, sometimes pureed, or raw in a green salad.

Salad burnet

French sorrel

Garden sorrel

Herb Mixtures

Bah Kuk tea: A blend of ten Chinese herbs and spices, used in soups. Available in sachets from Chinese supply stores.

Bouquet garni: The classic French "faggot" of aromatic herbs tied together and used to flavor stocks, soups and stews.

It usually consists of parsley, thyme and bay. The size of the bouquet varies according to the dish it is flavoring, as do the proportions used, although in the three-herb bouquet usually three-times as much parsley is used than the other two more aromatic herbs.

With certain dishes, other aromatic herbs are used, including rosemary, savory, celery, chervil, basil, tarragon and salad burnet. Lemon thyme is sometimes used in place of thyme. Pieces of orange peel (particularly favored in Provence), various spices and garlic may also be included in bouquet garnis.

The bouquet garni is tied by a long string to the pot handle so that it can be easily removed at the end of the cooking time. It is also a good idea to tie the herbs in a small piece of muslin, which can also hold the orange peel, garlic or spices if used.

Powdered bouquet garnis are sold widely; they are no substitute for the real thing, and nor are dried mixed herbs.

Having a constant fresh supply of the classic bouquet herbs at hand is very useful. They can be grown on a windowsill or outside the kitchen door in a single large pot, or as a group in smaller individual containers. It is worth growing more parsley then thyme, as it is used in greater quantity. A single bay tree should be more than sufficient.

Another pot, of the optional herbs, all of which are very important in their own right, could also be grown if there is space. It should include savory, chives, tarragon and chervil. Needless to say, a supply of fresh basil would also come in handy.

All the herbs mentioned are easy to grow, requiring only regular watering, feeding—and pruning.

Fines herbes: Another traditional French herb blend. Fines herbes comprises very finely chopped, subtly flavored herbs—usually parsley, tarragon, chervil and chives. Some recipes call for watercress and fennel leaves also, although the authenticity of these claims is disputed.

The classic use of fines herbes is for flavoring omelettes and egg dishes, but they are also much used with poached fish, chicken and a variety of vegetable dishes and as a garnish.

Herbes de Provence: A blend of typical dried herbs from Provence: thyme, rosemary, sage, marjoram, basil, fennel and mint. Used in stews and vegetable dishes.

Bah Kuk tea

Fines herbes

Herbes de Provence

Making bouquet garnis

Harvesting & Storing Herbs

Most herbs should be harvested just before they flower—their flavor is at its best then, before the seeds appear. Cut the herbs when the plant is completely dry. Cut back severely, as this is a good time to shape the plant.

Drying: Traditionally, herbs were tied into small bunches and hung upside down in a warm place, often over the stove. The drying can be done in the oven on its lowest setting, but care must be taken not to burn the leaves.

Storing: Once dried, the herbs can be sealed in paper or cloth bags; or they can be kept in tightly capped glass jars. In either case, store the herbs in a dark place—a drawer or cabinet, for instance.

Fresh herbs can be kept in glass jars in the refrigerator for several weeks without spoiling.

Freezing: Herbs can be frozen successfully, although they do tend to become rather limp when thawed.

The best way to preserve color and flavor is to tie the freshly harvested herbs in small manageable bunches and blanch for one minute, refresh under cold water, then leave to dry thoroughly. Place bunches in plastic bags and seal well so they are airtight. Turn the freezer to maximum and fast freeze the herbs.

Clove-pink

The Arabs have used the petals of the old-fashioned clove-pink *(Dianthus carophyllus)*, a tender perennial, as a flavoring for thousands of years. They were in fashion during the 17th and 18th centuries—in sauces, soups, wines, liqueurs and vinegars, and floated decoratively on chilled drinks.

They have a beautiful, spicy, clove-like taste and aroma. The petals can also be made into a syrup to flavor fruit dishes, or candied and eaten as a confection.

Geranium

There are over two hundred scented-leaved geraniums, all members not of the *Geranium* but of the tender *Pelargonium* family. The leaves are used fresh, to flavor and scent sweet dishes, creams and ice creams, custards and cakes.

The best-known variety is rose geranium *(P. capitatum)*, from which an oil, very similar to oil of roses, is extracted. Its leaves smell more of lemons when young, but age—the larger the leaf the stronger the taste—and cooking brings out the full rose flavor.

One or two leaves of the lemon-scented geranium *(P. monium)* are enough to flavor a jelly, custard or rice pudding. The leaves of the peppermint-scented geranium *(P. tomentosum)* are often used in apple jellies, and there is even a coconut-flavored geranium *(P. enoussular-oides)*. Other types include the apple-scented geranium *(P. odoratissimum)*, which smells strongly of apples, and the spicy nutmeg-scented geranium *(P. fragrans)*.

Geranium leaves lose their flavor when dry, so use fresh leaves.

Hibiscus

The beautiful red hibiscus flower used as a flavoring is produced by *Hibiscus sabdariffa,* an annual which grows in regions with hot climates such as India, Africa and the southern United States. It is also known as roselle.

The aromatic flowers, which have a slight lemon tang, are dried and floated on iced drinks and punches and used to flavor sauces and jellies. They are also often used in chutneys and curries in India and Southeast Asia.

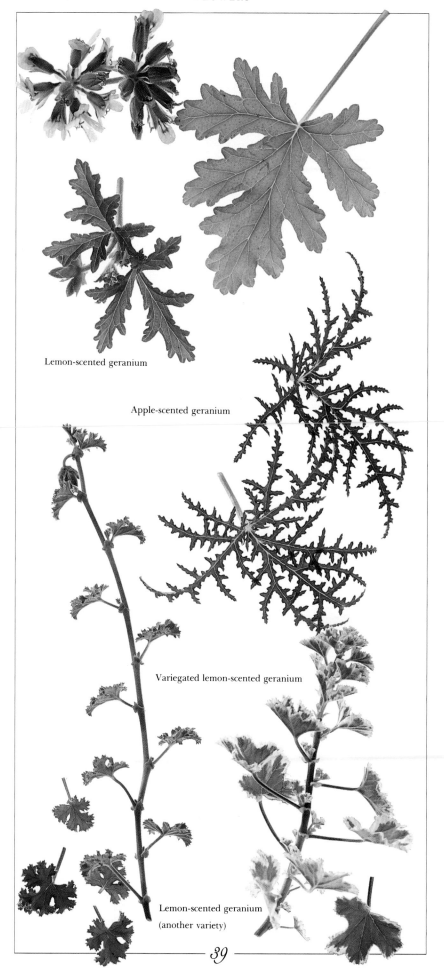

Lemon-scented geranium

Apple-scented geranium

Variegated lemon-scented geranium

Lemon-scented geranium
(another variety)

Elderflower

Lavender

Elderflower

The white flowers of the hardy deciduous elder tree *(Sambucus nigra* or *canadensis)* have a bitter, spicy taste when raw. But made into wine, they become mellow and grape-like; the best elderflower wines are fragrant, with a dryness and fruity quality which is superb. Elderflowers are also made into a light sparkling "champagne." The better known wines made from elderberries do not have the same subtlety.

Elderflowers are also used in jellies and fruit dishes, often combined with gooseberries. In Europe they are coated in a batter and fried.

Lavender

In the past, lavender was widely used to flavor sweets, wines, teas and confections. Today, this perennial, which thrives in a sunny position, is slowly regaining its popularity in the kitchen. It is now mainly used in ice creams, custards, sorbets and mousses. The flavor of lavender comes from its aromatic oil, which is used in perfumery.

There are several varieties: the commonest are the purple-flowered English lavender *(Lavender vera)* and the paler French lavender *(L. dentata).* The leaves and flowers can be infused to make teas (see page 70). Sprigs of lavender make a lovely decoration for a sweet dish.

Marigold

Marigold *(Calendula officinalis)* is an annual which likes a sunny position. Its small, brilliant yellow-orange petals have been used as a substitute for saffron for centuries. They are very similar in color to that spice, but have quite a different flavor—mellow yet bitter.

Fresh or dried, marigold petals are used in soups and stews, for both color and flavor; they also make a spectacular garnish. Like saffron, they are added to rice dishes, puddings and cakes; they are also made into wines and, commercially, are used to color butter and cheeses.

Nasturtium

The most important culinary product of the nasturtium plant *(Tropaeolum majus)* is the pickled flower bud, which is an excellent substitute for capers.

The orange, trumpet-like flowers of this sun-loving annual are also eaten: as a dramatic ingredient in salads, or stuffed with a sweet or savory filling. The leaves have a peppery taste and are also used in salads.

Marigold

Nasturtium

Primrose

The flowers of the primrose make a pretty addition to a salad, or they can be crystallized like violets. The primrose is another of the common garden flowers whose culinary uses have been long neglected. Apart from their decorative uses, the flowers can also be made into wine, and the young, bright green leaves are eaten as a salad. The yellow flowering primrose *(Primula vulgaris)* is a moisture-loving perennial.

Rose

Roses are a favorite flavoring in the Middle East. Rose water, made from the extracted essential oil, is sprinkled on sweets such as lokum, on rice puddings and pilafs, and used to flavor refreshing summer cordials. Sweet jams and jellies are made out of the scented petals.

In the West the petals are candied and used for decoration. They are also used to flavor honeys, syrups and vinegars.

The petals of any scented rose can be used for culinary purposes.

Violet

The leaves and flowers of the hardy sweet violet *(Viola odorata)* are very aromatic, and as extract of violets, obtained by infusion, is used for flavoring liqueurs, chocolates and candies as well as sweet dishes.

The heart-shaped leaves can be added raw to a salad, and so can the pretty purple flowers; however, they are often candied, as a confection.

Violets

Roses

Allspice

The Spanish introduced allspice (*Pimenta dìoica*) to Europe in the 16th century, calling it Jamaica pepper, after the place where it was found. Its name is confusing: it is not a mixture of spices, but is called allspice because it has an aroma and flavor reminiscent of cinnamon, nutmeg and cloves.

Allspice is the berry of an evergreen tree belonging to the myrtle family—a native of the West Indies and Central and South America. The berries are picked before they ripen and then sun-dried. They should be stored whole and ground when needed, as they tend to lose their flavor quickly.

Allspice is used generously in the Middle East, West Indies and Central America for spicing fish, meat and vegetables. Northern and Eastern Europeans use it mainly for pickling fish and meat. It is also used in marinades and chutneys, cakes and plum puddings and rice dishes.

Anise

Although unrelated botanically, there are three plants which share the name "anise." Two of them—anise and star-anise—contain the same essential oil, "anethole" (which is also found in fennel), and have a similar licorice-like flavor.

Anise (*Pimpinella anisum*) is grown mainly for the seed. It is a sun-loving annual, native to the Levant, which grows to 2 feet. Its yellowish-white flowers are followed by small oval seeds; these have been used for culinary and medicinal purposes for centuries.

Anise is still used in medicine for digestive complaints and is an ingredient in cough medicines. The seed is widely used to flavor breads, cakes, pastries and candies. In north and east Europe, it is added to cheese and cooked with vegetables such as cabbage. Aniseed, and indeed any of the anise-flavored liqueurs, have a particular affinity with fish; a small glass of Anisette or Pernod is often added to mayonnaise and served with lobster.

Star-anise, or badiane (*Illicium verum*), is a native of China, an evergreen of the magnolia family. The star-shaped fruit are dried and form an essential ingredient in many Chinese pork and duck recipes.

The third anise plant—anise pepper (*Xanthoxylum piperitium*)—is hot and aromatic. It is used mainly in China. With star-anise, cloves, fennel seed and cassis, it makes up the Chinese five-spice powder.

Annatto

The fragrant seeds of the annatto tree (*Bixa orellana*), a native of tropical America and the Caribbean, are also known as achiote. An important ingredient in Mexican cooking, the hard seeds are ground into a paste and used to color and flavor meats and fish; it is available in stores selling Latin American and Caribbean food.

In the Caribbean and some Latin American countries the hard yellowish-red pulp surrounding the seeds is used to make oil, which is added to meat, poultry and fish dishes. The same pulp is used in Europe to color cheeses, including Münster, Livarot and Maroilles.

Asafoetida

When the stems of this large, unpleasant-smelling plant (*Ferula asafoetida*) are cut, a milky liquid is produced. Dried, it turns into a brown resinous gum, which is used extensively in Indian cooking. Asafoetida is also available as a powder. It has a delicious, truffle-like flavor when cooked. Only minute quantities are needed.

Allspice

Star anise

Anise seeds

Anise pepper

Annatto

Asafoetida

Caraway

The caraway plant *(Carum carvi)* is a biennial which grows wild all over Europe and as far east as India, its country of origin. It also thrives in Northern Africa and North America. Most of the commercial crop comes from the Netherlands and eastern Europe. The most widely used part of the plant is the brown crescent-shaped seed, which has a flavor reminiscent of licorice, with a slightly bitter but pleasant aftertaste.

Caraway seed in one of the oldest known spices; its name comes from the ancient Arabic word *karawya.* It is widely used today in northern and central European and Jewish cookery but, interestingly, is almost unknown in Indian cooking.

Caraway seeds are used in fruit dishes, to flavor cakes, bread and cheese, and in savory dishes such as goulash and sauerkraut. The Hungarians make an "invalid's" caraway soup, while in Germany and Austria caraway is popular as a flavoring for root vegetables and is often added to sausages and pork dishes. With cumin, it is the flavoring of the liqueur Kümmel. Caraway seeds make a simple but excellent snack sprinkled thickly over buttered toast with salt.

The young feathery leaves are similar to dill weed and were once used in soups and salads. The roots can be boiled and eaten as a vegetable.

Cardamom

The cardamom plant *(Elettaria cardamomum),* a member of the ginger family, is a perennial which grows to about 8 feet in its native India. It is prized for its seeds. The pale green or brown seed pods hold small black, sticky seeds which contain volatile and fixed oil, starch, salt of potassium, mucilage, ash and resin. They have a strong, almost lemony taste and aroma. One of the most expensive and highly flavored of all spices, the seeds are sold in their pod, which is sometimes bleached white.

Cardamom is an extremely important spice in Indian cooking, being an essential ingredient of curries and pilaus, and bean and vegetable dishes. It is sometimes used whole in opened pods but more often ground.

It is also a favorite spice of the Arabs, who flavor coffee with it, and is widely used in northern and eastern Europe in cakes and pastries, and as a pickling spice. The essential oil is an ingredient in several liqueurs.

It is better to store pods whole, rather than buy the spice ready ground, as it loses flavor rapidly.

Cayenne

The reddish-orange powder called cayenne pepper is produced by grinding the dried seeds of two members of the Capsicum family, *C frutescens* and *C. Frutescens minimum.* It is extremely hot, with a sharp, almost burning taste and a slightly bitter smell.

Cayenne is an excellent spice to use for adding zest to dishes such as those containing cheese and eggs, although, of course, it must be used sparingly. It also goes well with fish and shellfish, and is often used as a condiment sprinkled on oysters, crab and lobster dishes.

Celery Seed

The brownish seeds of the celery plant *(Apium graveolens)* are often dried and used to flavor soups, stews and breads. They are a common addition to tomato juice. Much more popular twenty years ago than they are today, the seeds can be bitter if used to excess.

Caraway seeds

White cardamom pods

Green cardamom pods

Brown cardamom pods

Celery seeds

Cayenne pepper

Chilies

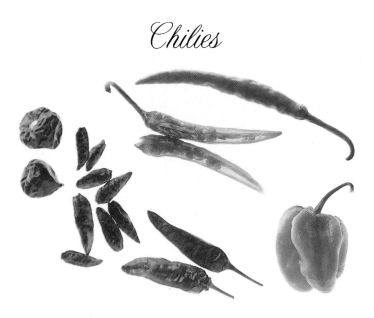

Chili peppers, red peppers, sweet or bell peppers, paprika and cayenne pepper all come from *Capsicum annuum* or *C. frutescens*, the same family to which the tomato, potato and eggplant belong. Many capsicum species grow wild in South America, particularly in Brazil, and there is evidence of their cultivation 9,000 years ago in the Valley of Mexico.

Chilies seem most prized in countries with hot climates. In Central and South America, the Middle East, India, Africa, Southeast Asia and Szechuan in China, chilies are used in all kinds of dishes: with vegetables, in meat and fish dishes, for sauces, pickles and salads. They are dried, pounded into powders and pastes and made into sauces and chutneys.

Chilies are used sparingly in Europe; only in the Mediterranean, in parts of Italy, Greece and Spain do they appear regularly.

Chili peppers grow in all shapes, color and sizes: they can be red, yellow, green, cream and black-purple, elongated or triangular, tiny and round. Unfortunately, there is no easy way to distinguish between those which are sweet and mild and those that are violently hot. Indeed, chilies from the same plant can vary in intensity from mild to extremely hot. And it is not always true that red chilies are riper and hotter than green ones. The only thing to do is taste them. (Always wash your hands immediately after handling chilies—it can be extremely painful getting the juice in the eyes.)

It is possible, however, to classify chilies into two groups: fresh and dried. Most are known in Western countries by their Mexican names, or simply as a "chili."

Dried chilies

Ancho: the ripened and dried poblano, deep reddish-brown in color and about 3" x 5", varies from mild to very hot.

Mulato: looks similar to the ancho but is brownish-black, slightly more wrinkled and sweeter.

Pasilla or **negro:** brownish-black, about 6" x 1"; very hot and rich.

Chipotle: light-brown and smoked, and *morita* are both extremely hot.

Fresh chilies

Serrano: about 1-1/2 inches long, tapering, smooth-skinned, medium green; quite hot.

Jalapeño: slightly darker and larger, 2-1/2 inches long; quite hot; available canned.

Malaguetta: tiny hot Brazilian pepper; a larger one, sometimes called cayenne chili, is widely available. Both sometimes sold ripe, when they are red and slightly less hot.

Scotch Bonnet: a West Indian lantern-shaped pepper, about 1-1/2 inches long with exquisite, fiery flavor, known as habañero in Mexico; sold canned.

Hari Mirch: hot green peppers used in India, 2 to 4 inches long.

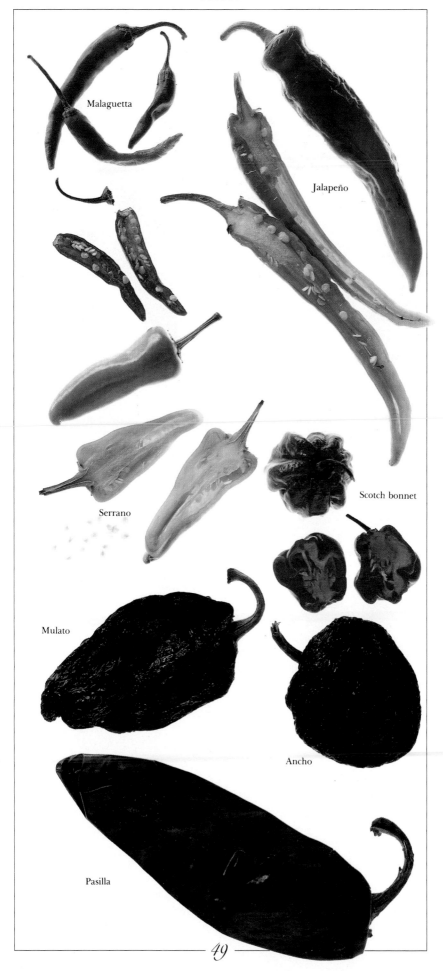

Malaguetta

Jalapeño

Serrano

Scotch bonnet

Mulato

Ancho

Pasilla

Cinnamon

Cinnamon sticks

Cloves

Ground cinnamon

Cassia sticks and ground cassia

The bark of a low-growing, ever-green bush *(Cinnamomum zeylanicum)*, this spice is native to Sri Lanka. It is peeled from thin branches in strips and, when dried in the sun, one strip inside the other, curls up into the familar quills. The finest quality cinnamon quills are pale and come from the thinnest bark.

Cassia *(Cinnamomum cassia)* is often confused with the true cinnamon: it comes from the same family, is sold in similar quills, and has the familiar cinnamon flavor and aroma, but it is stronger and slightly bitter. It has been used in China since 2500BC and is known as Chinese cinnamon.

Cinnamon is more expensive than cassia and the ground spices are often mixed together and sold as cinnamon; cassia powder is redder than true cinnamon. The ground spice loses its flavor quickly and should be bought in small quantities and stored in an airtight container.

Both spices are used extensively to flavor the meat dishes of the Middle East and the curries and rice dishes of India and Asia. In the Middle Ages, cinnamon was used in Europe as a condiment but was usurped by pepper and relegated to the sweet course; it is rarely used in European savory dishes today.

Cinnamon is a particularly good spice to use with chocolate or coffee and, of course, is widely used in cakes, cookies, fruit dishes, custards and spiced wines.

Ground cassia is one of the spices in the Chinese five-spice powder. The leaves of the cassia bush are widely used in India.

Clove

The name clove comes from *clavus,* the Latin word for nail, the shape of which the spice closely resembles. The clove tree *(Eugenia aromatica),* a member of the myrtle family and native of Southeast Asia, grows to 30 feet and flourishes only in tropical climates near the sea.

The spice is the young unopened flower bud. It is dried, when it turns a red-brown color and becomes one of the strongest spices. It should be used with discretion as it can easily overpower other flavors in a dish. One of the most popular spices, it is used in curries, sauces and stocks, in apple dishes, pickles and spiced wines and with baked ham and pickled fish. It is one of the spices included in garam masala.

Coriander

Coriander *(Coriandrum sativum)* is grown both for its leaves (see page 10) and seeds. In Thailand, the root is harvested as well and used with garlic and other spices. Coriander seeds have a milder flavor than the leaves and taste quite different. They are sweet and have a slight citrus taste. The seeds vary in color from pale green to cream or brown.

Whole coriander seeds are often used with fish, in sausages, breads and cakes and as a pickling spice. Ground, when it loses its flavor rapidly, coriander flavors roasted meat and is an essential curry spice. In India it is usually lightly roasted before being ground.

Cumin

Cumin seeds are produced by *Cuminum cyminum,* a delicate annual which originated in the East and flourishes only in hot climates. They are often confused with caraway, as they are slightly similar in shape. But they are quite different in taste: cumin has a mellower flavor, without the bitterness of caraway. Nevertheless, it is an extremely pungent spice and does tend to dominate any dish in which it is included. It is used in the blending of curry and chili powders.

Cumin is widely used in Indian cooking, and not just in curries, although it is one of the most characteristic of the curry spices. The seeds are used whole and ground, sometimes being roasted before they are ground. Black cumin seeds, which are said to have a more refined flavor, are also used, but they are relatively expensive.

Cumin seeds appear, too, in North African (notably in couscous dishes) and Mexican cooking, and sometimes in European food—for instance, to flavor sausages with cabbage dishes, in breads and also in Dutch Edam and German Munster cheeses. Cumin is an ingredient of Kümmel, a liqueur.

Dill

The buff-colored seeds of the dill plant *(Anethum graveolens)* are used as a spice and the feathery leaves are used as a herb (see page 12). Dill seeds taste a little like caraway and are used in similar ways—with cabbage, in root vegetable dishes, to flavor soups and stews and cheese and egg dishes.

The best known commerical use of dill is with pickled gherkins and cucumbers. Wine vinegars combined with dill are excellent (see page 66).

Coriander seeds

Black cumin seeds

Buff-colored cumin seeds

Dill seeds

Fennel Seed

Fennel seeds are harvested from the sweet fennel herb *(Foeniculum vulgare)* (see page 26) or from Florence fennel *(F. vulgare dulce)*, the low-growing variety cultivated for its bulbous stem which is eaten as a vegetable. Fennel seeds are used all over the world, mainly for medicinal purposes: they are reputed to be a good digestive and used in baby drinks.

Fennel seeds are sometimes included in curries or used to flavor breads and cakes. They are particularly noted for their inclusion in Italian sausages. Fennel seeds are also added to fruit tarts and liqueurs, and they are made into a tea.

Fenugreek

The plant *(Trigonella foenumgraceium)* originates in the Mediterranean region. The flat yellow seeds come from long pods which are produced in late summer, after the fragrant cream flowers have bloomed.

The name fenugreek comes from *fenum graecum,* the Latin for "Greek hay." According to evidence found in the Pyramids, it was used by the Egyptians.

The seeds have a faint curry flavor, with a bitter aftertaste. Their best known use is in Indian curries, but they are also used as a spice in the Mediterranean region and are widely used in Iran and Yemen, where they are often ground to a paste and added to vegetable dishes and savory sauces. Ground fenugreek seeds are also used in *halvah,* the popular Middle Eastern sweet. An excellent way to use whole fenugreek seeds is sprouted in salads.

The small oval leaves are cooked as a vegetable in India, Iran and Yemen. They are bitter and are best cooked with spices.

Fennel seeds

Fenugreek

Ginger

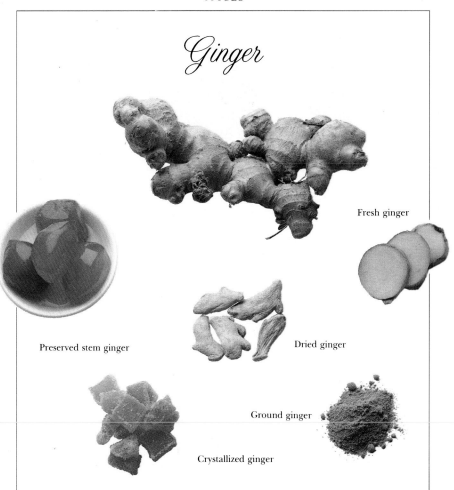

Fresh ginger

Preserved stem ginger

Dried ginger

Ground ginger

Crystallized ginger

The flower of the ginger plant *(Zingiber officinale)*—pale yellow and orchid-like—is as wondrous as the spice produced by its fat, irregular-shaped rhizomes. A native of the damp tropical jungles of Southeast Asia, ginger was one of the earliest spices imported into Europe over the caravan routes. The Spaniards introduced it to the West Indies in the 16th century, and today it is grown in all of the hot countries.

In Europe, ginger was regarded as an essential ingredient in most meat dishes until the 18th century. It then lost favor, and now is used almost exclusively in sweet dishes: breads, cakes, cookies, sweet sauces, custards, ice creams, with fruit, in pickles and in ginger beers and wines. Preserved ginger in syrup and crystallized ginger are served as sweetmeats. In contrast, ginger is used throughout India and Asia in savory dishes and in curries.

Ginger is available fresh or dried.

Fresh ginger: The rhizome (also known as a "hand" or "race") should be plump and firm. It must always be peeled and is then either finely chopped or pounded. The taste is sharp yet subtle; and its crispness is retained if lightly cooked.

The Chinese candy the fresh rhizome or preserve it in syrup for use as a confection. The best quality preserved ginger, "stem" ginger, is made from the youngest shoots and contains very little fiber; the syrup is used to flavor sweet dishes. Fresh ginger can be preserved in alcohol.

Dried ginger: Black or green ginger is produced by drying the unpeeled rhizome. White ginger, which is blanched, peeled and bleached before being dried, has a better flavor. Green ginger is the essential ingredient in some ginger wines. Dried ginger should be bruised with a rolling-pin or hammer to release the aromatic flavor during cooking and be discarded before serving.

Ground ginger: This is made from the dried rhizome. Like most spices, once ground, ginger loses its flavor; it is better to keep whole dried ginger and grind some when required.

| Grains of paradise | Juniper berries | Mace |

Grains of Paradise

This spice comes from the small brown seeds contained in the fruit of the West African tree *Amomum melegueta*, which is a family member of ginger and cardamom. Grains of paradise are widely used in the Caribbean and in Africa; they are also called Melegueta or Guinea pepper. The flavor is hot, spicy and aromatic. The spice was previously widely used instead of pepper. It is obtainable from West Indian or African grocers or can be replaced with allspice.

Juniper

This plump, dark blue-purple berry grows on a spiky-leaved bush (*Juniperus communis*), which thrives in the woods and mountain gullies of Mediterranean Europe. It takes three years to ripen fully and is strongly aromatic and sweet.

Although juniper is used as a flavoring all over Europe, particularly in northern European countries and in the Mediterranean region (where the berries are oilier and therefore stronger in taste), it is not as widely favored as it ought to be.

Juniper has a special affinity with venison and other robust game meats, and is used in marinades, stuffings, sauces and pâtés; it is also excellent with pork and chicken. It can be added to meat stews, is a common ingredient in sauerkraut, and is occasionally used to flavor apples and pears. It is the prevailing flavor in gin, and is an ingredient in a number of other spirits, including aquavit and schnapps, and in some beers.

Before using, the berries should be crushed to bring out the taste and aroma. Because their flavor depends on the quantity of essential oil they contain, they cannot be dried successfully and are never sold ground. The oil is said to be a cure for digestive and kidney complaints.

Mace

Mace comes from the same fruit as the nutmeg (*Myristica frgrans*) (see page 56); it is the scarlet skin, or aril, which surrounds the nutmeg seed. Once removed, it is flattened and dried, becoming quite brittle. This time-consuming process to produce what are called "blades of mace," and the finer flavor of the product, makes this spice much more expensive than nutmeg, although the flavor of the two is similar.

Mace is used in similar ways too: in stews, sweet dishes, cakes and sauces, with fish, meats—particularly veal and chicken—and vegetables. It is also good to use in an infusion to flavor creams, in poaching liquid, and in clear stocks—the appearance of which would be spoiled by grated nutmeg.

Because it is rather expensive, ground mace is often adulterated. Like most spices, it tends to lose its potency quickly.

Mustard

Brown mustard seeds

English dry mustard

Black mustard seeds

Bordeaux mustard

Dijon mustard

German mustard

The flavor and pungency of mustard is due to a hot-tasting oil contained in the mustard seed, which is only released when the crushed seed is mixed with cold liquid.

There are several types of mustard plant; the principal ones grown for seed are *Brassica nigra,* which produces reddish-black seeds, *B. juncea* or brown mustard, and *Sinapis alba,* a white-seeded variety.

Nigra mustard, a native of the Middle East, is the most pungent of the three and, until very recently, was the most commonly used. But it is a difficult plant to harvest mechanically and has therefore been largely replaced by the more manageable, but less pungent, juncea mustard. The alba variety, known as white or yellow mustard, is very much weaker and is used in combination with juncea.

Mustard seed is used in Indian cooking, usually lightly roasted. Elsewhere it is sold in powdered form or mixed into a paste.

Dry mustard: The most famous of these is English mustard. It is made by grinding the seed and passing it through a fine sieve. It contains juncea mustard, often mixed with white mustard. It should be mixed with cold water and set aside for at least ten minutes to allow the flavor to develop. It can then be mixed with vinegar or lemon juice, both of which stop the development process, or added to hot dishes. English mustard is served with roast beef, sausages, ham and other cold meats, and is added to sauces.

Mixed mustards: Of the mixed mustards, the two most common French ones are Dijon and Bordeaux. Dijon has long been a center of mustard production. The pale preparation made in Dijon under appellation control is based on nigra or juncea mustard seeds (alba seeds are not permitted), which are hulled and ground with verjuice. Dijon mustard has a light, sharp taste, hot and slightly salty, and is regarded as finer than Bordeaux. It is the "classic" mustard, used in sauces and mayonnaises.

Bordeaux mustard is darker. The seed coats are not removed; it is mixed with vinegar and sugar, and flavored with tarragon.

German mustards are similar to those of Bordeaux—dark and flavored with herbs and spices. They are used in the spicy meat dishes of Germany and northern Europe.

American mustards are usually made with alba seeds and are fairly mild in flavor. They are excellent with barbecued meats and hot dogs.

There are many other mustards available, flavored with garlic, peppercorns, pimento, and so on.

Nigella

Nigella is used as a spice in the Middle East and India. The tear-shaped black seeds grow on a small plant *Nigella sativa*. Aromatic with a peppery taste, they are sometimes used instead of pepper.

In India, where they are called "Kalonji," nigella seeds are used as a pickling spice, sprinkled on breads, and added to fish and vegetable dishes by the Bengalese. The seeds are also used in Egypt.

Nigella is sometimes called fennel flour or devil-in-the-bush. In France the seeds are occasionally included in *quatre-épices* instead of pepper.

Nutmeg

The nutmeg comes from a large evergreen *(Myristica fragrans)* native to the Malucca Islands in Indonesia. It was introduced to Europe by the Portuguese in the 16th century. Once the fleshy yellow fruit has ripened and dried, it splits open. Inside, enclosing the nutmeg seeds, is the scarlet aril which is removed and dried to become mace (page 54).

The hard brown nuts are never used whole but are finely grated; freshly grated nutmeg is far superior to the powdered variety.

Nutmeg is used extensively in Italy and the Middle East. As well as flavoring cakes and puddings, it is used with meats and vegetables—notably spinach, lamb and sausages—in sauces and with cheese.

Paprika

Paprika is a Hungarian word and paprika pepper is the national spice of Hungary, where over six different kinds of the finely ground powder are available. They range in color from the brightest red to a light rose, and in flavor from light, sweet and spicy to fiercely sharp.

Paprika is made from dried and ground red peppers *(Capsicum tetragonum)*. Its pungency depends on the proportion of flesh to seeds used.

Sadly, much of the paprika sold outside Hungary is of inferior quality and it is rare to find many varieties.

Depending on its hotness, paprika can be used in generous quantities. The Hungarians use it extensively—in soups, vegetable, meat, chicken and fish dishes. It is the essential flavor of goulash.

Paprika also makes an attractive garnish—sprinkled over egg and cheese dishes and cream sauces.

Pepper

The vine peppers *(Piper nigrum)* which produce peppercorns are unrelated to the Capsicum family; they are members of the *Piperaceae* family and are native to the Malabar coast in Southeast India.

Vine pepers produce strings of berries which are pickled green and dried in the sun to become black peppercorns. Berries which are left to ripen, turn red; from these we get white peppercorns—the ripe berries are dried then soaked to remove the dark husk. Green peppercorns are the unripe berries pickled in brine; pink peppercorns are pickled ripe ones. A Chinese tree produces Szechuan peppercorns, which are reddish-brown and very hot; they are available whole and seeded.

Up until the 18th century, pepper was a valuable commodity, used to pay taxes, levies and rents.

Pepper is, of course, used extensively in almost every country: there are few savory dishes which it does not flavor. It is strongly aromatic and contains a resin which is responsible for its pungency. Black peppercorns are more aromatic but not as sharp as white ones. Like most spices, peppercorns should be bought whole and ground when needed; they keep indefinitely.

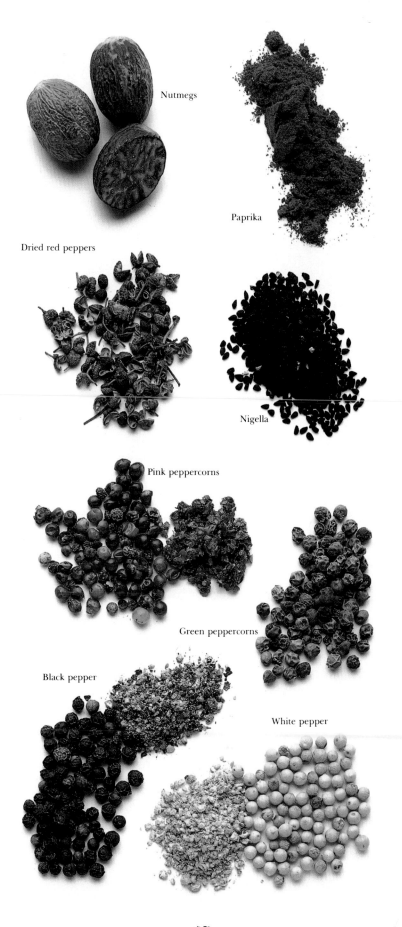

Nutmegs

Paprika

Dried red peppers

Nigella

Pink peppercorns

Green peppercorns

Black pepper

White pepper

Yellow-white poppy seeds

Black poppy seeds

Saffron threads

Powdered saffron

Poppy Seed

The spice known as poppy seed is the ripe seed of the opium poppy *(Papaver somniferum)*. The tiny blue-grey seeds, which have a nutty taste, are used extensively in European and Middle Eastern cookery, mainly in sweet dishes, to make cakes and strudel fillings, and sprinkled on breads. But they are also excellent with many vegetables. Noodles flavored with the seed are eaten in central Europe.

The poppy seeds used in India, called *khas khas*, are yellow-white. Used whole or ground, they are added to savory as well as sweet dishes; they often take the place of a thickening agent.

Saffron

Saffron is almost as expensive as gold. It is the dried stigmas of a blue-flowered crocus *(Crocus sativus)* which are hand picked and sold as the spice. It is variously estimated that between 200,000 and half a million stigmas are needed to make 2 pounds of saffron, which accounts for its price.

The saffron crocus, a member of the Iris family, is a native of Turkey and surrounding countries; it should not be confused with the unrelated autumn crocus *(Colchicum autumnale)* which is poisonous.

Saffron has a slightly bitter flavor and a dark orange-gold color; it is used both to color and flavor dishes. Fortunately, very little is required; it can be bought in "threads" or ground. Because it is so expensive, saffron has always been adulterated, so it is best to buy the threads, which should be dark orange with no white streaks. Safflower stigmas, which are redder and lack the characteristic flavor, are often sold as saffron.

Saffron has been used in food since ancient times. It is an essential ingredient in *bouillabaisse, paella* and *risotto milanese,* and is used in all kinds of fish and shellfish dishes, in sauces, rice dishes and soups. Saffron cakes date as far back as the Middle Ages.

Before using, saffron threads should be broken up and infused in hot liquid; strain the liquid into the dish. Powdered saffron is also infused before use.

Turmeric (see page 60), with its different taste and less subtle color, is no substitute for saffron.

Sesame Seed

The tiny creamy-colored seeds from the sesame plant *(Sesamum indicum)* are one of the world's oldest spices. They are also the source of a valuable cooking oil, used extensively in India, Asia and Central America, and commercially in margarine production.

The seeds have a sweet nutty taste and are used—lightly roasted—sprinkled on breads, cakes and vegetables. The ground seeds are made into *halvah*, the grainy confection of the Middle East. They are also pounded into a creamy paste, called *tahini*, which is used from Greece to Syria and Jordan, mixed with yogurt and garlic as a sauce for vegetables and salads, and with honey for fruit salads.

Black sesame seeds are used in Japanese cooking, usually roasted first. Sesame oil is also popular there, but it is stronger as it is made from the roasted seeds.

Sumac

Sumac seeds are used in the Middle East, particularly in Lebanon, as a souring agent in place of lemon juice.

There are over 250 species of sumac, but it is only the Sicilian sumac *(Rhus corioria)* that is widely used in cooking: in fact, many of the other species are poisonous. The sour seeds are dried, then crushed and steeped in water to extract their juice. Sumac can also be bought in powder form, which is added directly to dishes.

A North American species, *R. glabra*, produces red berries which the Indians use to make a cordial; they have a similar sour quality.

Roasted sesame seeds

Cream-colored sesame seeds

Black sesame seeds

Sesame oil

Sumac

Tamarind

Tamarind is the large dark brown pod produced by the tamarind tree *(Tamarindus indica)*, a native of eastern Asia. It thrives in tropical climates all throughout Asia, the Indian subcontinent, the Middle East, Africa and the West Indies.

The seed pod, which is ripened on the tree, contains a fleshy pulp which accounts for its sourness. The pods are sold whole, then broken and soaked. The pulp is extracted in the form of juice and the seeds and the pods are then discarded.

Known also as the "date of India," it is widely used in Indian and Southeast Asian cooking, as well as in Iraq and the Gulf States, and in Africa—in curries, chutneys and pickles, and in refreshing drinks—as a souring agent.

Tamarind paste is also widely available: this is the compressed pods minus the seeds; it needs to be soaked before use. Usually a little sugar is added to the soaking liquid.

Turmeric

A relation of the ginger plant, turmeric *(Curcuma longa)* has much broader leaves, although it is rather similar in looks. Like ginger, the spice is obtained from the rhizome, the flesh of which is a brilliant orange. The rhizomes are dried, then peeled and ground. Turmeric is almost always sold as a powder as the fresh rhizome is difficult to grind.

The color is the reason for turmeric's importance: it is used as a coloring agent in curries, pickles, rice dishes, drinks and sweet dishes. However, it does have a distinctive taste: fragrant, faintly curry-like and slightly bitter. Turmeric is also used extensively for commercial purposes to color such foods as mustards, butter and cheese. It is mainly used in the East, particularly in India, China and Indonesia, and in Morocco and the West Indies.

Turmeric should never be substituted for saffron: the color and the flavor are quite different.

Vanilla

Vanilla was first cultivated by the Indians of Mexico, who used it to flavor chocolate. It is reputed to have been introduced into the eastern United States by Thomas Jefferson, who on return from France missed vanilla ice cream. The vanilla sold as a spice is the pod of the climbing orchid *Vanilla planifolia,* which comes from the east coast of South America and grows only in tropical climates.

The orchid produces white flowers followed by long yellow pods. The pods are picked unripe and fermented to bring out the familiar delicate, spicy flavor.

The finest vanilla has a smooth black surface, is between 8 to 12 inches long, and is covered with a frost of the vanillin crystals from which the taste and aroma are derived. Inferior vanilla pods are dull, lighter in color and usually shorter with little or no frosting.

Vanilla extract is also widely available, produced by extracting the flavor from crushed vanilla pods with alcohol. Because it is possible to produce vanillin synthetically, many adulterated products are sold as vanilla extract; the true extract is not cheap.

Vanilla extract is often used to flavor cakes and meringues, and has wide commercial applications.

Chocolate and vanilla is an Aztec combination, much used today in commercial chocolate-making. Vanilla is used extensively to flavor cream desserts, custards, ice creams, cakes, rice puddings, soufflés and mousses. The vanilla pods are usually infused in the cream mixture and removed before cooking; they are carefully washed and dried.

Keeping a vanilla pod in the sugar jar for vanilla sugar is a well-known use. Vanilla pods should be stored in an airtight container in a dark place.

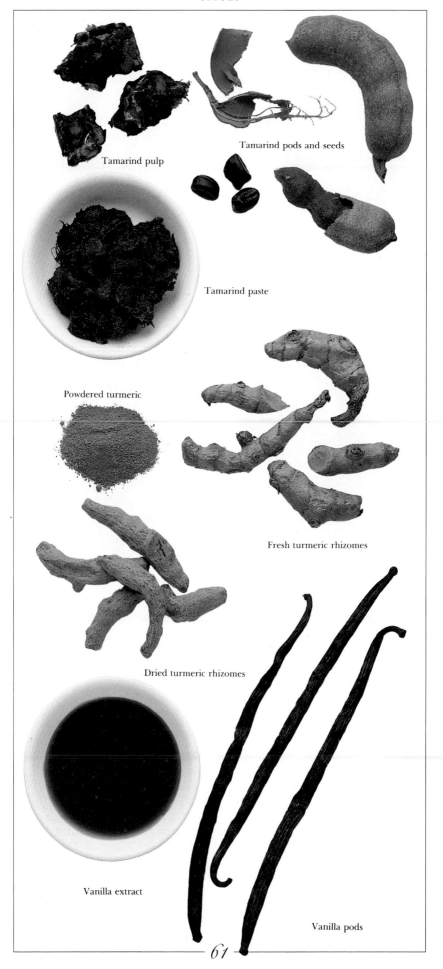

Tamarind pulp

Tamarind pods and seeds

Tamarind paste

Powdered turmeric

Fresh turmeric rhizomes

Dried turmeric rhizomes

Vanilla extract

Vanilla pods

Alino criolo

Curry powder

Japanese seven-flavor spice

Indian five-spice powder

Pickling spice

Spice Mixtures

Alino criolo: A Venezuelan mixture of garlic salt, ground annatto seeds, chopped oregano, ground cumin, paprika, and a little black pepper; garlic is added when used. In Latin America, it is added to stews.

Curry powder: Not used in India, where spices for curries are always blended at home, but often used for convenience elsewhere. The ingredients always include some of the following: cloves, cinnamon, ginger, nutmeg, black pepper, chili, coriander seed, fenugreek, cumin, mustard seed, poppy seed, turmeric, cardamom and curry leaf, which is the main feature of a Madras curry.

Chinese five-spice powder: An aromatic mixture of ground star anise, fennel seed, cassia, cloves and Szechuan pepper. Widely used in China and other parts of Asia on fruit dishes and to flavor all manner of stews, particularly red-cooked meat.

Garam masala: Indian mixture used as condiment. Contains various spices which usually include cumin seed, peppercorns, cloves, coriander seed, cardamom and cinnamon. The spices are dry-roasted individually and ground. Often mixed at home, there are as many recipes as there are people in India.

Chinese five-spice powder

Garam masala

Quatre-épices

Sambal

Indian five-spice powder: A bengali mixture of whole spices added at the beginning of cooking, or ground and used as a condiment. Contains cumin seed, fennel seed, fenugreek seed, nigella seed and radhunio, a tiny aromatic spice which resembles (and is often replaced by) black mustard seed.

Japanese seven-flavors spice: Includes dried tangerine peel, pepper leaf, sesame seed, poppy seed, rape seed and hemp seed; pungency varies according to proportions. Used as a condiment on rice and noodles and as a garnish.

Pickling spice: An English mixture which varies according to where it is bought, but usually contains mustard seed, allspice, coriander seed, hot chilies, bay leaves and dry ginger tied in muslin. It is used for spicing chutneys, relishes and fruits.

Quatre-épices: A French mixture containing four spices: nutmeg, cloves, cinnamon or ginger, pepper or nigella. Used to flavor sausages and pâtés, with baked ham and roast pork.

Sambal: Indian and Chinese hot pickle-type mixture, containing chilies, sugar, salt, oil, lemon juice, onions; sometimes dried shrimp and lemon grass are added. It is usually made at home and eaten as a relish with most meats.

Garlic

The most controversial of all flavorings, garlic is loved by most of the world and seems to repulse the rest—mainly Anglo-Saxons and vampires!

Garlic *(Allium sativum)* is a native of central Asia but is not naturalized all over the world. It is a member of the onion family, which is reflected in its name, from the Old English *gar* (lance) and *leac* (leek). Grown for its bulb, the plant has flat slender leaves and white flower heads.

There are many garlic varieties: the bulbs—or heads as they are also called—vary in the size and number of cloves they contain, and some have white skin, others pink or mauve skin. The garlic grown in hot climates tends to be the sweetest of all with the best flavor.

Garlic should be hard and full, with no discolored spots, and it is best stored in a cool place. Its flavor can vary from sweet and nutty to strong and pungent. Whether it is eaten raw or cooked affects the taste, as does the method of cooking. A soup made from two or three heads of garlic, or meat roasted with forty cloves, will have a surprising fragrance and mellowness; half a clove added raw to a salad will be stronger and much more pungent; and fried garlic is different still. Many dishes, particularly in Catalonia and the French Pyrenees, are based on this difference and combine raw and cooked garlic.

An easy way to peel a garlic clove is to squash it with the blade of a heavy knife to loosen the skin before peeling. When dealing with large numbers of cloves, the best method is to simmer them in gently boiling water for several minutes—the skins can then be slipped off.

Worshipped for its curative and preventative powers by the Egyptians, and used to great effect during the plague, garlic contains antiseptic substances which work on the digestive system; it is also said to relieve coughs and colds, and reduce blood pressure. It has been used as a stimulant and is also said to counteract the effects of alcohol and rich food.

These benefits are great, but the proof of the garlic is in the eating. There are a vast number of dishes which depend on garlic for their flavor. It is used in everyday cooking in all parts of the world, with the exception of the Anglo-Saxon and north European countries. In fact, garlic is an indispensable part of all the great cuisines, from Japan and China, through Thailand, India, the Arab countries, eastern Europe, to the shores of the Mediterranean and Italy, France and Spain.

It is included in every kind of savory dish, with meat, poultry, game, fish, shellfish and vegetables. It is sautéed with onions, blended with spices, mixed with fresh herbs, used to flavor sauces, made into soups, and even baked whole and served as a vegetable.

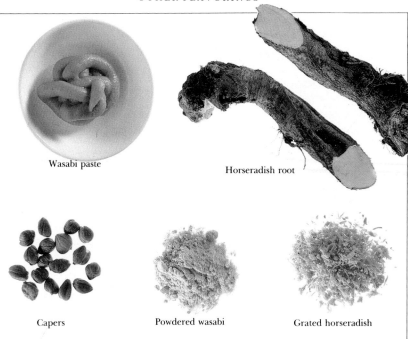

Wasabi paste

Horseradish root

Capers

Powdered wasabi

Grated horseradish

Horseradish

The horseradish plant *(Armoracia rusticana)* is a hardy perennial with large waxy-edged leaves and a thick brown tap-root which is off-white inside. It is the root which is eaten, as a condiment, in sauces and salads.

Horseradish is very pungent with a sharp and biting flavor, although it loses much of its piquancy when cooked or added to hot dishes. It is used extensively in its native eastern Europe and in northern Europe, often in sauces which include vinegar or cream and are traditionally served with roast beef, smoked fish and egg salads; it also goes well with ham and sausages. Mayonnaise can be flavored with the grated root, and the French use it to make an interesting sauce that contains bread crumbs, cream and vinegar.

Good commercial horseradish creams are widely available. Horseradish can also be bought dried.

There is also a Japanese horseradish called *wasabi*. It is used freshly grated and is stronger than the European variety. It is often sold dried and pounded into a pale green powder. Like powdered mustard, it is mixed with water and left to stand before using. It is very hot and should be used very sparingly, with fish and in sushi.

Capers

Capers have been used in the kitchen for thousands of years—they are even mentioned in the Old Testament. They are the unopened flower buds of the trailing shrub *Capparis spinosa*, which grows wild all around the Mediterranean basin and in North Africa. Consequently, capers figure prominently in the cuisine of these areas.

The shrub has tough ovate leaves and large white flowers with four petals. The buds contain an organic acid, caprio, which only comes out when they have been pickled in vinegar or dry-salted, and gives their characteristic flavor. Usually sold in small jars, capers must be kept covered with the pickling liquid.

Capers have many uses. They go well with fish and cold meats, and are essential in fresh herb sauces, sauce tartar, caper sauce, *tapenade*—the olive paste of the Mediterranean— and in the Sardinian salad of eggplant and tuna called *caponata*. They are often used with olives and garlic in fish dishes, tarts and pizzas, and make a superb spaghetti sauce, chopped with anchovies, garlic and parsley, and as a garnish.

Flavored Vinegars

Vinegars and oils steeped with herbs and spices are an excellent way of flavoring salads. They can also be used in mayonnaises and a variety of sauces.

To make flavored vinegars, the herb or spice is steeped in white wine vinegar; sometimes the vinegar is heated before the flavoring ingredient is added. The bottle must be tightly capped and left in a sunny place for two to three weeks. At this point, vinegars containing seeds and chopped herbs are generally strained (see individual vinegars below). The vinegars should then be stored in a cool, dark place.

Quantites for 2-1/2 cups white wine vinegar are:

Basil vinegar: 14 tablespoons pounded basil in heated vinegar; strain.
Bay leaf vinegar: 10 fresh bay leaves in heated vinegar.
Coriander-seed vinegar: 3 tablespoons cracked coriander seed; strain.
Dill vinegar: 2 tablespoons dill seed, 1 ounce fresh dill leaves; strain.
Elderflower vinegar: 3-1/2 ounces elderflowers; strain.
Fennel vinegar: 2 tablespoons fennel seed, 6 tablespoons fennel leaves; strain.
Garlic vinegar: 4 large cloves crushed garlic; strain.
Herb vinegar: 1/2 ounce each tarragon, chervil, borage and watercress leaves, 2 cloves crushed garlic, 1 dried chili; strain.
Hot chili vinegar: 6 hot red chilies, 1 clove crushed garlic; strain.
Lavender vinegar: 1 ounce lavender flowers; strain.
Lemon-balm vinegar: 1 ounce chopped lemon balm; strain.
Marjoram vinegar: 1 ounce chopped marjoram; strain.
Mustard-seed vinegar: 3 tablespoons cracked mustard seed; strain.
Rose-petal vinegar: 3-1/2 ounces rose petals; strain.
Rosemary vinegar: 2 medium-size stems of rosemary.
Salad-burnet vinegar: 1 ounce chopped salad-burnet leaves; strain.
Spiced vinegar: 1 teaspoon black peppercorns, 1 teaspoon finely chopped gingerroot, 1 teaspoon celery seed and 1 teaspoon allspice, with 1 dried chili pepper and 1 cinnamon stick. Simmer vinegar with spices; strain.
Tarragon vinegar: 2 medium-size stems of tarragon.

Flavored Oils

These are not as common as vinegars, but they are excellent. They do not need to be strained before using.
Basil oil: Pound 6 tablespoons basil. Using 2-1/2 cups olive oil, gradually add a little oil as for mayonnaise; once 1/4 cup oil has been amalgamated, mix with the remaining oil and pour into a jar. Cap tightly and store for three weeks before using.
Rosemary oil: To a 24-ounce bottle of olive oil, add 4 stems of rosemary, and 2 cloves garlic, halved. Cap tightly and store for three weeks before using.
Spicy oil: To a 24-ounce bottle of olive oil, add 2 cloves garlic, halved, 6 fresh chilies, 8 black peppercorns, 8 juniper berries, 8 sprigs of lemon thyme and 2 stems of rosemary. Cap tightly and store for three weeks before using.

Dill vinegar

Rose-petal vinegar

Tarragon vinegar

Spicy oil

Basil oil

Rosemary oil

Savory Butters

A classic way of using herbs and spices is in savory butters, which are very easy to make: cream the butter, add the flavoring, season to taste, then form into a roll and chill. To serve, cut in 1/2-inch slices. Savory butters can be frozen.

Quantities given are for 1/2 cup creamed butter:

Chive butter: 4 ounces chives, pounded. For grilled fish and meat.

Chivry or ravigote butter: 1 ounce each chives, parsley, tarragon, salad burnet and chervil, blanched, dried and pounded. For cold dishes.

Colbert: 1 ounce each tarragon and parsley, and juice of 1/2 lemon. For grilled fish and meat.

Cumin-seed butter: 1-1/2 teaspoons cumin seed. For cheese and vegetable dishes.

Garlic butter: 4 cloves garlic, minced. For cold dishes, grilled meats.

Green butter: 8 ounces raw spinach, pounded and squeezed dry. For poultry, cold dishes.

Horseradish butter: 1-1/2 ounces horseradish, finely grated. For grilled meats and fish.

Chive butter

Chivry butter

Colbert

Cumin-seed butter

Garlic butter

Green butter

Juniper butter

Horseradish butter

Juniper butter: 10 juniper berries, crushed. For grilled meats.

Maître d'hôtel butter: 1 ounce parsley, chopped, 1/2 teaspoon salt, dash lemon juice. For grilled fish and meat, fried fish and vegetables.

Montpellier butter: 1/2 ounce each parsley, chervil, watercress, tarragon, chives and spinach: 1 shallot, finely chopped, blanched and squeezed dry; pounded with 1 clove garlic, 1 tablespoon plus 1 teaspoon capers, 4 anchovy fillets, yolks of 3 hard-boiled eggs. For cold dishes, especially fish, on croûtons.

Mustard butter: 1 tablespoon plus 1 teaspoon French mustard. For grilled fish and meat, cold dishes.

Paprika butter: 1-1/2 teaspoons paprika. For poultry and canapés.

Parsley butter: 2 ounces parsley, pounded. For grilled fish and meat.

Shallot butter: 8 finely chopped shallots. For grilled fish and meats.

Sweet cicely butter: 1-1/2 ounces sweet cicely, pounded. For poultry and fish.

Tarragon butter: 2 ounces tarragon, blanched and pounded. For poultry, cold dishes and canapés.

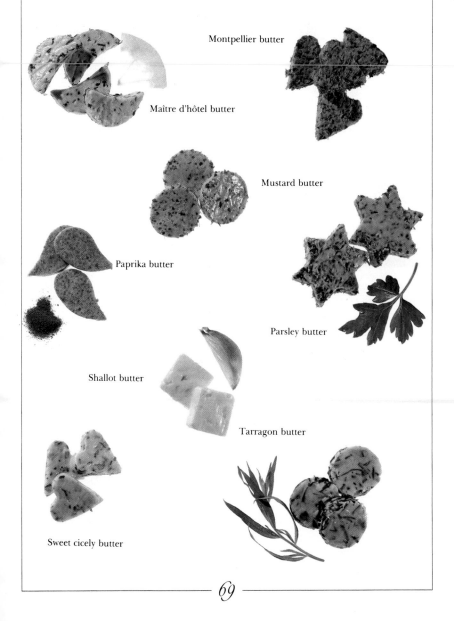

Montpellier butter

Maître d'hôtel butter

Mustard butter

Paprika butter

Parsley butter

Shallot butter

Tarragon butter

Sweet cicely butter

Teas

Flavored teas, also called tisanes, are made by infusing fresh or dried herbs, or spices, in boiling water. They are extremely varied and can be naturally sweet, or bitter and sweetened with honey, or sharpened with lemon juice, and served hot or chilled. Many have a long history as medicinal cures.

Quantities given are for 1 pot of tea, about 5 cups, unless otherwise stated.

Angelica tea: 6 dried angelica leaves; infuse for 5 minutes, strain.

Bergamot tea: Add 3 to 4 fresh bergamot leaves or 1 tablespoon plus 1 teaspoon dried bergamot flowers to pot of ordinary tea; infuse for 5 minutes; strain.

Cinnamon tea: Add 2 cinnamon sticks to pot of ordinary tea; strain.

Elderflower soda: 8 to 10 elderflowers, 1/4 cup superfine sugar, juice and peel of 1 lemon; pour over 3 cups boiling water and stir. Serve hot or chilled, strained.

Fennel tea: 1 tablespoon bruised fennel seeds; infuse for 5 minutes, strain. Sweeten with honey to taste.

Juniper tea: 20 crushed juniper berries; infuse for 10 minutes, then strain and sweeten to taste.

Lemon-balm tea: 1 tablespoon plus 1 teaspoon dried lemon balm leaves; infuse for 5 minutes, strain. Sweeten to taste.

Lovage tea: 1 tablespoon plus 1 teaspoon dried lovage leaves; infuse for 5 minutes, strain and season with salt to taste.

Mint tea: 1 tablespoon plus 1 teaspoon dried mint leaves; infuse for 5 minutes, strain, add 1 tablespoon plus 1 teaspoon sugar and cool. Before serving, add juice of 1 lemon.

Peppermint tea: 1 tablespoon crushed fresh peppermint leaves; infuse for 5 minutes, then strain and sweeten to taste.

Rosemary tea: 4 sprigs of rosemary; infuse for 5 minutes; then strain.

Sage-leaf tea: 2 teaspoons each fresh chopped sage and lemon balm, 2 lemon wedges, 1 tablespoon sugar; infuse for 5 minutes, strain, cool, then add 2/3 cup white wine.

Thyme tea: 8 sprigs of thyme leaves and flowers; infuse for 10 minutes, then strain.

Angelica

Cinnamon and tea leaves

Fennel with honey

Thyme leaves and flowers

Juniper berries

Rosemary sprigs

Sage, lemon balm and lemon

Watercress Soup with Marigolds

2/3 cup garbanzo beans
3 thyme sprigs
3 tablespoons olive oil
1 leek, finely chopped
2 zucchini, cubed
1 carrot, sliced
2 tablespoons finely chopped
  parsley
4-1/2 cups chicken stock
3 cups finely chopped watercress

To Garnish:
3 marigold flowers

Put garbanzo beans in a bowl, cover with cold water and let soak 2 hours. Put into a large saucepan with soaking liquid and thyme. Add water to cover beans by about 4 inches. Bring to a boil and boil steadily 10 minutes. Lower heat, cover pan and simmer 30 to 40 minutes or until soft. Drain beans and discard thyme.

In another saucepan, heat oil. Add leek, zucchini, carrot, parsley and beans. Cover and cook over gentle heat 10 minutes to soften vegetables. Pour on chicken stock and simmer 15 to 20 minutes or until vegetables are tender. Add watercress.

Puree soup in a blender or food processor until smooth. If too thick, thin with a little hot chicken stock.

Serve immediately, garnished with marigold petals.

Makes 6 servings.

Potato & Herb Soup

1 tablespoon butter
1-1/2 lbs. potatoes, cubed
1-3/4 cups chicken stock
1-3/4 cups milk
Salt and pepper to taste
1 egg yolk, if desired
1/4 cup finely chopped mixed
  seasonal herbs
1 tablespoon whipping cream, if
  desired

To Garnish:
Parsley sprigs or other herbs

In a large saucepan, melt butter over low heat. Add potatoes, cover and let stand 5 minutes to allow potatoes to absorb butter.

In another saucepan, heat chicken stock and milk; pour over potatoes and season with salt and pepper. Simmer gently, stirring occasionally, about 15 minutes or until potatoes are cooked.

The soup is equally good served hot or chilled. If it is to be served hot, return to pan and reheat gently. Beat egg yolk in a soup tureen, then gradually add hot soup. Sprinkle with chopped herbs and swirl in cream, if desired. Garnish with herbs and serve immediately.

If soup is to be chilled, pour into a tureen and chill until required. Add cream, if desired, and herbs just before serving.

Makes 4 servings.

Note: Use four or five different herbs, including a balance between the sharper varieties such as thyme, and mellower flavors—basil and parsley—for example.

Goat Cheese with Mint

6 ozs. goat cheese
1/3 cup milk
1 tablespoon olive oil
1 teaspoon lemon juice
1/2 red bell pepper, seeded
4 teaspoons chopped mint
Salt and pepper to taste

To Garnish:
Mint sprigs

To Serve:
Crackers, if desired

Press goat cheese through a nylon sieve into a bowl. Add milk, oil and lemon juice and blend well until mixture is smooth and creamy. Cut bell pepper in thin strips 2 inches long. Fold into cheese mixture with chopped mint. Season with salt and pepper.

Mold cheese mixture into a flat round 6-inch dish. Place on a serving plate, cover with plastic wrap and chill at least 4 hours to allow flavors to mingle.

Uncover cheese and garnish with mint sprigs. Serve with crackers, if desired.

Makes 4 servings.

Note: A delicious starter which may alternatively be served at end of meal in place of cheese.

For a more decorative effect, mold cheese in a heart or diamond shape.

Smoked Salmon Parcels

8 ozs. smoked salmon
2 (3-oz.) pkgs. cream cheese,
  softened
2 tablespoons olive oil
2 teaspoons lime juice
3 tablespoons finely chopped dill
  weed
Black pepper to taste
4 teaspoons horseradish cream

To Garnish:
Lime slices
Dill sprigs

Lightly oil 4 (1/3-cup) ramekin dishes. Line each with smoked salmon, molding it to fit dish and leaving a little extra to fold over top of dish.

Blend cream cheese with oil and lime juice. Add chopped dill, black pepper and any extra smoked salmon, chopped. Spoon in horseradish, but do not mix in thoroughly; it should be distributed in hot ribbons throughout cream cheese mixture.

Place 4 to 5 teaspoons of cream cheese mixture in each ramekin, then fold smoked salmon over top to make a parcel. Chill 3 to 4 hours.

To serve, turn out onto a plate. Garnish with lime slices and dill.

Makes 4 servings.

Note: A less elaborate way of serving this starter is to spread cream cheese mixture over strips of smoked salmon and roll them up to make cornets.

Prosciutto & Sage Crespellini

4 slices prosciutto, cut in half
8 large sage leaves
2 eggs
3/4 cup all-purpose flour
Pinch salt
1/3 cup milk
Vegetable oil for frying

Wine Sauce:
1/4 cup butter
1 tablespoon all-purpose flour
1/3 cup white wine
Salt and pepper to taste
4 teaspoons whipping cream
3 tablespoons grated Parmesan
  cheese

Tomato Sauce:
2 teaspoons olive oil
8 ozs. tomatoes, skinned, seeded,
  chopped
1 garlic clove, crushed
Salt and pepper to taste

To make crespellini, mix eggs, flour, salt and milk in a blender or food processor. Chill 1 to 2 hours.

Heat oil in a crepe pan. Using 2 tablespoons batter, tilt pan to spread batter. Cook on both sides. Makes 8 crespellini.

To make wine sauce, melt butter. Add flour and cook, stirring, 1 to 2 minutes to form a roux. Add warm wine, stirring. Season and simmer 20 minutes, stirring occasionally. Remove from heat and stir in cream and Parmesan.

Meanwhile, prepare tomato sauce. Heat oil and add remaining ingredients. Simmer 15 to 20 minutes.

Preheat oven to 350F (175C). Cover bottom of a baking dish with a thin layer of wine sauce. Place a half slice of prosciutto, a sage leaf and 2 teaspoons tomato sauce on each crespellini. Fold over and place in baking dish. Pour over remaining wine sauce and bake 15 minutes.

Makes 4 servings.

Gnocchi with Tamarillo & Basil

Gnocchi:
2 lbs. potatoes, boiled
1-3/4 cups all-purpose flour
1/2 teaspoon salt
1 teaspoon white peppercorns, ground
2 egg yolks
1/4 cup butter, cut in pieces

Sauce:
1-1/4 lbs. tamarillos
1 tablespoon olive oil
2 shallots, finely chopped
Salt and pepper to taste
1 tablespoon chopped basil leaves

To Garnish:
Basil leaves

To Serve:
Grated Parmesan cheese

To prepare gnocchi, mash potatoes with a potato masher (not in a blender or food processor—it makes them too gluey). Put into a bowl and gradually sift in flour, salt and white pepper, blending in well with a wooden spoon. Beat in egg yolks and butter, then knead until mixture is well blended; it should feel light and elastic.

On a lightly floured surface, roll out a handful of mixture to a 3/4-inch circle. Shape by folding over side of a fork; it will curl up into a shell. Repeat with remaining mixture. Set aside until ready to cook.

To make sauce, cut tamarillos in half, spoon out flesh and chop. In a saucepan, heat oil, add shallots and cook a few minutes to soften. Add tamarillos and seasoning; simmer until thick. Remove from heat and stir in basil. Spread a layer of sauce in bottom of a serving dish; keep warm.

Cook gnocchi in a large saucepan of boiling salted water 3 to 4 minutes—they are ready when they rise to top. Remove with a slotted spoon and place in serving dish. Cover with remaining sauce and sprinkle with basil leaves. Serve with Parmesan cheese.

Makes 4 to 5 servings.

Eggplant Terrine

1 (2-lb.) eggplant, halved
2 teaspoons olive oil
1 garlic clove, crushed
2 tablespoons all-purpose flour
1/2 cup fromage frais
3 eggs
2 ozs. Parmesan cheese, grated
2 ozs. provolone piccante or other
   mature hard cheese, grated
Salt and pepper to taste
1 small red bell pepper, peeled
   (see page 108), finely chopped
1 tablespoon finely chopped basil

Tomato Sauce:
1 tablespoon olive oil
1-1/2 lbs. tomatoes, peeled,
   seeded, chopped
Salt and pepper to taste

To Garnish:
Basil leaves

Preheat oven to 375F (190C). Put eggplant cut side down on a baking sheet and bake about 45 minutes or until soft. Cool. Lower temperature to 350F (175C).

Peel eggplant, mash flesh and squeeze out moisture. Place flesh in a blender or food processor with oil, garlic, flour, fromage frais, eggs and cheeses; blend until smooth. Add salt and pepper.

Butter a 5-cup terrine dish and line with buttered waxed paper. Pour in 1/2 of eggplant mixture and smooth. Cover with chopped bell pepper and basil, then remaining eggplant mixture. Smooth top and cover dish tightly with foil. Place in a large dish or roasting pan in 1 inch of water. Bake in oven 55 to 60 minutes or until terrine is firm to touch. Cool, then chill several hours.

To make tomato sauce, in a saucepan, heat oil. Add tomatoes and salt and pepper to taste. Cook gently 15 to 20 minutes or until thick; cool.

To serve, turn terrine onto a serving plate and cut in slices. Garnish with basil leaves and serve with tomato sauce.

Makes 6 servings.

Sorrel Tart

Pastry:
1-3/4 cups all-purpose flour
1/2 teaspoon salt
7 tablespoons butter, cut in small
  pieces
1 egg yolk
About 1/3 cup chilled water

Filling:
2 tablespoons olive oil
2 large onions, sliced
2 teaspoons light-brown sugar
1 lb. sorrel
1 teaspoon salt
1/3 cup whipping cream
Pinch grated nutmeg

To Garnish:
Parsley sprigs

To prepare pastry: sift flour and salt into large bowl. Cut in butter until mixture resembles bread crumbs, then add egg yolk with water. Work together using finger tips until mixture forms a firm smooth dough. Wrap in plastic wrap and chill several hours.

Preheat oven to 400F (205C). On a lightly floured surface, roll out pastry thinly and line a 9-inch flan dish. Fill pastry with dried beans and bake blind in oven 10 to 15 minutes, until lightly colored. Lower temperature to 375F (190C).

To prepare filling, in a skillet, heat oil. Add onions and sugar and cook gently about 15 minutes to soften.

Meanwhile, in a large un-covered saucepan, cook sorrel, with water clinging to leaves after washing, and salt 10 minutes until reduced and moisture has evapo-rated. Drain well and chop coarsely.

Place onions in crust. Cover with sorrel, pour over cream and season with nutmeg. Bake in oven 30 minutes. Serve hot or cold, gar-nished with parsley.

Makes 6 first-course servings or 4 main-course servings.

Gail's Artichokes

4 artichokes
1 lemon

Bread Crumb Stuffing:
1 cup dried bread crumbs
1/2 cup grated Parmesan cheese
4 teaspoons caraway seeds
1/2 teaspoon salt

Shrimp Stuffing:
1/3 cup olive oil
6 ozs. shrimp, peeled, deveined,
    chopped
1 shallot, finely sliced
2 teaspoons capers
1 tablespoon chopped parsley

To Garnish:
Parsley sprigs

Wash artichokes thoroughly in several changes of water; drain. Trim leaves and scoop out choke, rub cut surfaces with lemon.

To prepare bread crumb stuffing, mix together bread crumbs, Parmesan cheese, caraway seeds and salt.

To prepare shrimp stuffing, in a small saucepan, heat 1 tablespoon oil and fry shrimp, shallot, capers and parsley a few minutes.

Put a spoonful of shrimp stuffing in the center of each artichoke; fill gaps between leaves with bread crumb stuffing. Put artichokes in a saucepan large enough to hold them tightly in a single layer. Pour over remaining olive oil. Add 1 inch of water, cover pan tightly and cook 1-1/4 hours or until artichokes are tender.

Carefully lift out artichokes. Drain thoroughly and serve immediately, garnished with parsley sprigs.

Makes 4 servings.

Variation: Aniseed or fennel seeds may be used instead of caraway seeds.

Chicken Livers & Fennel

2 tablespoons butter
1 small fennel bulb, thinly sliced
2 shallots, finely chopped
8 ozs. chicken livers, each cut in
   4 to 6 pieces
2 teaspoons dry sherry
1 tablespoon chopped walnuts
Salt and pepper to taste
2 teaspoons chopped fennel
   leaves

Croûtes:
4 thin slices bread, crusts
   removed
Melted butter

To Garnish:
Fennel leaves

Preheat oven to 375F (190C).

To prepare croûtes, cut bread in half diagonally. Brush both sides with melted butter. Place on a baking sheet and bake in oven about 10 minutes, until golden.

Meanwhile, in a skillet, melt butter. Add fennel and shallots and saute until fennel is beginning to brown. Remove vegetables with a slotted spoon and keep warm.

Add chicken livers to skillet and cook about 4 minutes—they should remain pink inside. Push to one side of pan. Add sherry and stir into cooking juices, then cook rapidly about 1 minute. Lower heat and return fennel and shallots to pan. Add walnuts and stir in chicken livers, seasoning and chopped fennel leaves.

Spoon chicken livers and fennel onto croûtes and serve immediately, garnished with fennel leaves.

Makes 4 servings.

Note: If fennel leaves are unavailable, use feathery tops of fennel bulb or substitute dill weed.

Leek & Mussel Omelette

3 tablespoons olive oil
1 shallot, finely chopped
Salt and pepper to taste
2/3 cup white wine
1 lb. mussels, cleaned
8 ozs. leeks, thinly sliced
8 eggs
1/4 cup butter
2 tablespoons chopped chervil

To Garnish:
Chervil sprigs

In a large saucepan, heat 1 tablespoon olive oil. Add shallot and 1/2 teaspoon salt and cook a few minutes to soften. Pour in wine and add mussels. Cover and cook about 5 minutes, until mussels open; discard any that do not. Remove mussels with a slotted spoon and shell; discard shells. Strain cooking liquid through muslin twice. Return liquid to pan and boil rapidly until reduced by half; set aside.

In a clean pan, heat remaining oil. Add leeks and cook gently 10 to 12 minutes, until soft. Add mussels and 2 teaspoons reduced cooking liquid. Check seasoning and heat through.

Meanwhile, prepare 4 (2-egg) omelettes. For each one: beat 2 eggs with salt and pepper. In a preheated omelette pan, melt 1 tablespoon butter until sizzling. Add eggs and cook until browned underneath but soft and creamy on top.

Spread 1/4 of filling on 1/2 of omelette. Sprinkle with 1/4 of chopped chervil and fold omelette over to cover. Serve immediately, garnished with sprigs of chervil.

Makes 4 servings.

Note: To clean mussels, scrub thoroughly under cold water, removing beards and discarding any with open or broken shells.

Lobster & Fennel Salad

2-1/2 cups pasta shells
1 tablespoon olive oil
Salt and black pepper to taste
6 ozs. French green beans, cut in
   1-1/2-inch lengths
1 red bell pepper, cut in
   1-1/2-inch lengths
1 fennel bulb, thinly sliced
3 small lobsters, cooked
5 teaspoons snipped chives

Mayonnaise:
2 egg yolks
2 teaspoons lemon juice
1/4 teaspoon salt
About 1-1/4 cups olive oil
1 tablespoon Anisette or Pernod

To Garnish:
Few chives

Cook pasta shells in boiling salted water until *al dente;* drain and put in a salad bowl. Add 1 tablespoon oil, salt and pepper and toss well. Cool.

Prepare mayonnaise in usual way, adding Anisette or Pernod once oil has been incorporated into egg yolks. Check seasoning.

Blanch green beans, then refresh under cold water to set color. Drain and place on top of pasta shells. Season lightly. Arrange bell pepper over green beans; season lightly. Top with fennel slices; season lightly.

Remove lobster meat from shells and shred; set claws aside. Add lobster meat to salad and sprinkle with chopped chives. Garnish with lobster claws and chives. Serve with mayonnaise.

Makes 4 servings.

Note: Anise-flavored mayonnaise goes equally well with crab and crayfish, and is a more interesting sauce to serve with shellfish than a simple vinaigrette or mayonnaise.

Shrimp with Fenugreek & Ginger

1 teaspoon fenugreek seed
1/3 cup grapeseed oil
2 teaspoons finely chopped
    gingerroot
1 garlic clove, finely chopped
1/2 cup dried bread crumbs
12 raw jumbo shrimp, peeled,
    deveined
1/2 teaspoon salt
Black pepper to taste

To Serve:
Lemon slices
Salad leaves

Bruise fenugreek seed in a mortar.
    In a small saucepan, heat oil over low heat. Add fenugreek and gingerroot and saute over very low heat 10 minutes, taking care spices do not burn. Remove from heat and add garlic and bread crumbs.
    Place shrimp in a bowl. Pour over oil and bread crumb mixture, making sure shrimp are well coated. Season with salt and pepper. Refrigerate at least 2 hours at room temperature, turning shrimp at least once.
    Preheat grill on high setting until very hot.
    Meanwhile, thread 3 shrimp onto each of 4 skewers. Cook shrimp 2 minutes on each side on very hot grill; they must be watched carefully as fenugreek has an unpleasant bitter flavor if burnt.
    Serve immediately on lemon slices with salad leaves.

Makes 4 servings.

Variations: Lemon grass can be added for extra flavor. Peel and finely chop 2 stalks of lemon grass; add to marinade mixture with garlic and bread crumbs.

Scallop Seviche

1 lb. scallops
1/2 teaspoon salt
Juice 4 to 5 limes
1 small red bell pepper, seeded
1 fresh chili pepper, seeded,
  finely chopped
2 green onions, finely chopped
1 garlic clove, minced
1/2 oz. creamed coconut
1/4 cup whipping cream
2 tomatoes, sliced
2 avocados, sliced
2 tablespoons chopped cilantro

To Garnish:
Cilantro leaves

Put scallops into a bowl. Sprinkle with salt and pour over lime juice; scallops should be completely covered with juice. Cover bowl and chill 4 hours, turning scallops occasionally.

Slice bell pepper in fine strips; cut strips in 1-inch lengths. Add to scallops with chili, green onions and garlic. Return to refrigerator another hour.

In a small saucepan, break up creamed coconut with a wooden spoon until quite finely mashed. Add cream gradually and heat gently until smooth; cool.

Pour off lime juice, then add tomatoes and avocados to scallops. Pour over coconut cream and toss well. Check seasoning and add chopped cilantro.

Serve immediately, garnished with cilantro leaves.

Makes 4 servings.

Variation: Omit coconut cream sauce. Replace with a vinaigrette made from grapeseed oil and white wine vinegar.

Sole with Saffron & Chervil

2 tablespoons butter
4 lemon soles, filleted, skin and
  bones reserved

Fish Fumet:
2-1/2 cups water
1/2 onion, sliced
1 carrot, quartered
1 stalk celery
8 peppercorns
4 parsley sprigs
2 thyme sprigs
1 bay leaf

Saffron Sauce:
1 packet saffron
1 tablespoon boiling water
3 egg yolks
1/2 cup butter
2 tablespoons finely chopped
  chervil

To Garnish:
Salad leaves

To prepare fish fumet, in a large saucepan, put skin and bones from fish, water, onion, carrot, celery, peppercorns, parsley, thyme and bay leaf. Bring to a boil, then simmer gently 1 hour. Strain and reduce over high heat until about 1/4 remains. Set aside.

To make saffron sauce, infuse saffron in boiling water; strain and set liquid aside.

Combine egg yolks, fish fumet, butter and saffron liquid in top part of a double boiler or a bowl set over a pan of gently simmering water. Cook, whisking constantly, until thickened; do not allow water to get very hot. Just before serving, add chervil.

To cook fish, in a skillet, heat butter until almost smoking. Put in fish and fry several minutes on each side, until golden.

Serve immediately, garnished with salad leaves and accompanied by saffron sauce.

Makes 4 servings.

Gumbo with Okra

2 tablespoons butter
1/3 cup olive oil
2 onions, chopped
8 ozs. okra, sliced
2 stalks celery, sliced
2 garlic cloves, finely chopped
2 strips bacon, chopped
3 garlic sausages, cut in pieces
(about 12 ozs. total)
1 fresh chili pepper, seeded,
chopped
4 potatoes, cubed
2 tablespoons finely chopped
parsley
2 teaspoons chopped thyme
4 bay leaves
2-1/2 cups chicken stock
1-1/2 cups medium dry white
wine
Salt and pepper to taste
1 lb. cod fillets, cut in 1-inch
pieces
12 ozs. clams
Pinch cayenne pepper, if desired

To Garnish:
Chopped parsley

In a large flameproof casserole, heat butter and oil; add onions, okra, celery and garlic. Cover and cook over low heat for about 8 minutes or until vegetables have softened. Add bacon and sausages and cook until browned. Add chili, potatoes, parsley, thyme and bay leaves. Pour in chicken stock and wine and add salt and pepper. Simmer 20 to 30 minutes or until potatoes are cooked. Add cod and clams and cook 4 to 5 minutes, until fish is cooked. Check seasoning; add cayenne pepper, if desired. Discard bay leaves.

Garnish with parsley to serve.

Makes 6 servings.

Note: If desired, gumbo can be partly prepared in advance: when potatoes are cooked, cool and chill if necessary; skim. Reheat gently 15 minutes before serving. When simmering point is reached, add fish and continue as above.

Baked Fish Ravigote

5 lbs. red snapper or bass
2 garlic cloves, slivered
1 onion, sliced
1 teaspoon chopped thyme
3 bay leaves
Salt and pepper to taste
5 lettuce leaves
1-1/4 cups white wine

Sauce:
3/4 cup each finely chopped
   parsley, chervil, chives,
   tarragon and watercress
2 tablespoons chopped capers
4 anchovy fillets, chopped
1/3 cup olive oil
Juice 2 lemons
3 hard-cooked egg yolks,
   crumbled
Pepper to taste

To Garnish:
Lemon slices

Preheat oven to 375F (190C).

Make slits in skin of fish and insert garlic. Put in an oiled ovenproof dish and sprinkle with onion, thyme, bay leaves, salt and pepper. Cover with lettuce leaves and pour on wine. Cover and bake in oven 30 to 35 minutes or until fish is cooked. Carefully lift fish from dish and set aside to cool.

To make sauce, in a small bowl, combine herbs, capers and anchovies; mix in oil and lemon juice. Just before serving, add egg yolks and pepper.

Serve fish on a platter, garnished with lemon slices. Serve sauce separately.

Makes 6 to 8 servings.

Trout with Watercress

4 (12-oz.) trout, cleaned, boned
Salt and pepper to taste
3 cups coarsely chopped
   watercress
1 grapefruit, segmented, chopped
1/4 cup dried bread crumbs
Butter

Sauce:
3 tablespoons white wine
2 tablespoons cold water
3 egg yolks
Pinch salt
1 cup butter
3 cups coarsely chopped
   watercress

To Garnish:
Watercress sprigs

To prepare sauce, in a small sauce-pan, combine wine and cold water. Boil until reduced to 1 tablespoon and cool.

In top part of a double boiler or a bowl set over a pan of simmering water, beat reduced liquor into egg yolks and salt. Keeping water in bottom pan to a slow simmer, gradually beat in butter, about 2 tablespoons at a time. Keep warm.

Put watercress in a bowl of boiling water; let stand 3 minutes then strain. Squeeze out all moisture and pound, then pass through a sieve—there should be 3 to 4 tea-spoons puree. Set aside.

Preheat oven to 375F (190C). Season trout with salt and pepper. Fill each trout cavity with 1/4 of chopped watercress and grape-fruit and 1 tablespoon bread crumbs. Place each trout on a square of foil, put a pat of butter on top and wrap up. Place in an ovenproof dish and bake in oven 25 minutes or until fish is cooked. Unwrap and place on warmed serving plates.

Stir watercress puree into warm sauce. Garnish fish with water-cress and serve with sauce.

Makes 4 servings.

Fish Ragoût

**1 (2-1/2- to 3-lb) piece monkfish
or swordfish
Salt and pepper to taste
3 tablespoons olive oil**

Sauce:
**1 tablespoon olive oil
1 onion, chopped
1-1/2 cups chopped parsley
1 teaspoon chopped rosemary
2 teaspoons chopped thyme
2 bay leaves
2 tablespoons capers
2 tablespoons chopped black
olives
1 lb. tomatoes, skinned, seeded,
chopped
2/3 cup finely chopped walnuts
1 cup red wine**

Watercress Puree:
**2 tablespoons butter
1 lb. watercress**

To Garnish:
**Lemon slices
Watercress sprigs**

Preheat oven to 375F (190C).

Place fish in an ovenproof dish. Season with salt and pepper and pour over olive oil. Bake in oven about 40 minutes or until fish is cooked, basting occasionally.

To prepare sauce, in a large saucepan, heat olive oil. Add onion and saute until golden. Add herbs, capers, olives, tomatoes, walnuts and wine; simmer 30 minutes. Discard bay leaves. Puree in a blender or food processor; pour sauce over fish and return to oven 5 minutes.

To make watercress puree, in a small saucepan, melt butter. Add watercress and cook gently until softened. Puree in a blender or food processor, then season to taste.

Serve fish hot, garnished with lemon slices and watercress and accompanied by watercress puree.

Makes 6 servings.

Salmon with Dill & Mustard

4 (8-oz.) salmon steaks
Salt and pepper to taste
2 teaspoons olive oil

Sauce:
1 teaspoon salt
1 tablespoon sugar
1 teaspoon ground black pepper
1/2 teaspoon ground allspice
1/4 cup cognac
1/4 cup white wine
4 teaspoons Dijon-style mustard
2 tablespoons chopped dill weed

To Garnish:
Chicory
Curly endive

To prepare sauce, in a small sauce-pan, put salt, sugar, pepper, allspice, cognac and wine. Bring to a boil and boil vigorously until reduced by half. Strain and keep hot.

Preheat grill on high setting.

Season salmon steaks with salt and pepper. Place on lightly oiled foil and drizzle a little olive oil on top of each salmon steak. Fold foil to make a basket; do not close completely. Grill steaks 6 to 8 minutes, until cooked through and browned; there is no need to turn them over. Remove from foil and place on warmed serving plates.

Stir mustard and dill into hot sauce. Pour a spoonful over each steak. Garnish with chicory and curly endive to serve.

Makes 4 servings.

Note: Dill and mustard sauce can also be served with whole baked or grilled salmon. Increase sauce quantities according to weight of fish; note that amount of sauce per portion is quite small.

Saffron Chicken

1/4 cup plus 1 tablespoon boiling
 water
1 (3-inch) piece tamarind, shelled
1-1/2 teaspoons sugar
1-1/2 teaspoons salt
1 packet saffron
1 tablespoon boiling water
2 tablespoons vegetable oil
2 onions, sliced
4 (4-oz.) chicken breasts
1 (1-inch) piece gingerroot, finely
 chopped
4 garlic cloves, crushed
1 dried chili pepper, seeded,
 finely chopped
1-1/4 cups plain yogurt

To Garnish:
Few chives

Pour 1/4 cup boiling water over
tamarind and soak 3 to 4 hours.
Press tamarind liquid and pulp
through a sieve; discard any
fibrous residue. Mix tamarind
with sugar and 1/2 teaspoon salt.

Soak saffron in boiling water
about 30 minutes. Strain, reserving liquid.

In a large skillet, heat oil. Add
onions and cook until browned.
Add chicken breasts and cook until browned all over. Pour off oil
from pan; add gingerroot, garlic,
chili, yogurt and 1 teaspoon salt.
Cover and cook at a slow simmer
20 minutes.

Add prepared tamarind and
saffron to chicken. Cook, uncovered, over moderate heat 10
minutes, until sauce has reduced a
little, stirring occasionally. Garnish chicken with chives and serve
with saffron rice.

Make 4 servings.

Note: Tamarind imparts a sour
flavor; if it is unavailable, substitute juice of 1/2 lemon.

Stuffed Veal Rolls

1 lb. veal scallops
2 tablespoons butter
1 tablespoon olive oil
1/2 cup white wine
2 tablespoons finely chopped
  parsley

Stuffing:
1 cup dried bread crumbs
1/2 cup grated Parmesan cheese
2 teaspoons salt
1/2 cup finely chopped walnuts
6 tablespoons finely chopped
  parsley
Water

To Garnish:
Lemon wedges
Salad leaves

Pound veal until thin. Cut in small pieces, about 1-1/2 inches square.

To prepare stuffing, mix together bread crumbs, cheese, salt, walnuts and 6 tablespoons parsley; add a little water to moisten.

Place a little stuffing on each veal square and roll up tightly. Thread 3 rolls each onto 4 wooden skewers.

In a skillet, heat butter and oil. Cook veal rolls, turning occasionally, until golden and cooked through. Remove from skillet and keep warm.

Pour off any fat from skillet. Add wine and stir into pan sediment. Let sauce bubble 3 to 4 minutes. Just before serving, add 2 tablespoons parsley.

Pour sauce over veal rolls and serve immediately, garnished with lemon wedges and salad leaves.

Makes 4 servings.

Variation: Use stuffing for larger rolls. Allow 1 to 2 scallops per person and increase quantity of stuffing by half. Pound each scallop thinly, top with stuffing, roll up and secure with wooden picks. Cook as above.

Pork with Clams

2 tablespoons olive oil
1-1/2 lbs. boneless pork, cubed
2 onions, sliced
4 garlic cloves, crushed
1 tablespoon paprika
1 teaspoon salt
1 bay leaf
1-2/3 cups white wine
1 lb. tomatoes, peeled, seeded,
  chopped
1 lb. clams, cleaned
1 onion, finely chopped
1 tablespoon chopped parsley
Salt and pepper to taste
3 tablespoon chopped cilantro

To Garnish:
Cilantro sprigs

In a flameproof casserole, heat oil. Add pork and cook until evenly browned. Add sliced onions and garlic and cook until softened. Add paprika, salt, bay leaf, wine and tomatoes. Cover and simmer gently about 1-1/2 hours or until meat is tender.

Meanwhile, in a large saucepan, put clams, chopped onion and parsley. Cover with water. Bring to a boil, then simmer gently until clams are cooked. They will open and rise to surface—discard any that do not open. Drain and set aside.

Just before serving, add clams to pork and heat through 5 minutes. Add salt and pepper and discard bay leaf.

Sprinkle with chopped cilantro and garnish with sprigs of cilantro to serve.

Makes 4 servings.

Variation: For a simple, tasty alternative, omit clams and increase pork to 2 pounds.

Beef with Oregano

2 tablespoons olive oil
4 strips bacon
2 lbs. boneless beef round steak,
   cut in 10 to 12 pieces
2 onions, quartered
2 tablespoons finely chopped
   oregano
2 tablespoons finely chopped
   parsley
1 bay leaf
1 large garlic clove, crushed
1/2 cup red wine
1/3 cup water
1 cup chopped green olives
2 tablespoons fresh bread crumbs
Grated peel 1 lemon
Salt and pepper to taste

To Garnish:
Oregano sprigs

To Serve:
Fresh bread
Green salad

In a flameproof casserole large enough to place beef in 1 layer, heat oil. Add bacon and sauté until crisp; remove with a slotted spoon and set aside. Add beef and cook until evenly browned. Add onions and toss in oil for 1 minute.

Add 1/2 of oregano and parsley, bay leaf, garlic, wine and water. Cover and simmer 2 hours. Add bacon and olives and continue cooking 45 minutes—the stew should be fairly liquid.

Mix together bread crumbs, lemon peel and remaining herbs and add to stew. Cook, uncovered, 10 to 15 minutes more. Season with salt and pepper. Discard bay leaf.

Garnish with oregano sprigs and serve with fresh bread and green salad.

Makes 4 servings.

Variation: Thyme can be added to this casserole for a stronger, more aromatic flavor. Substitute 1 tablespoon finely chopped thyme for 1/2 of oregano.

Lamb with Mustard & Tarragon

1 (4-lb.) boneless lamb shoulder
2 garlic cloves, slivered
4 teaspoons dry mustard
2 teaspoons salt
3 to 4 tarragon sprigs
Black pepper to taste
1 tablespoon olive oil
2 tablespoons butter
1 onion, finely sliced
3/4 cup white wine
1 tablespoon chopped tarragon

To Garnish:
Sprigs of tarragon

Preheat oven to 350F (175C).
Make several slits in lamb and insert garlic. Mix together mustard and salt and smear 1/2 of mixture on inside of lamb. Lay tarragon sprigs on lamb and season with black pepper. Roll up and secure with string. Rub outside of lamb with remaining mustard and salt mixture.

In a flameproof dish, heat oil and butter. Add lamb and brown on all sides. Add onion and cook for a few minutes to soften, then pour in wine. Stir and scrape up all juices and sediment. Cover and bake in oven 2-/12 to 3 hours, to desired doneness. Remove lamb from dish and let stand 10 minutes before serving.

Pour fat off cooking juices, then simmer several minutes, stirring constantly. Just before serving, remove string from lamb and carve. Add chopped tarraggon to sauce. Serve garnished with tarragon sprigs.

Makes 6 to 8 servings.

Note: Lamb shoulder is one of the best cuts to use for casseroles; it is lean and full of flavor. Ask the butcher to bone it for you—add bones to soup for extra flavor.

Spiced Lamb with Fruit

2 tablespoons olive oil
2 lbs. boneless lean lamb, cubed
1 onion, sliced
1 teaspoon each chopped sage,
   rosemary, thyme and marjoram
2 teaspoons fennel seeds
1/2 teaspoon fenugreek seeds,
   crushed
1 teaspoon ground coriander
1 teaspoon ground ginger
1 teaspoon ground turmeric
1 teaspoon ground mace
3 garlic cloves, crushed
1 lemon
1 orange
2 apples, peeled, cored, sliced
1 tablespoon honey
1/2 cup red wine
Salt and pepper to taste

To Garnish:
Orange and lemon slices
Rosemary sprigs

In a flameproof casserole, heat oil. Add lamb a litttle at a time and cook until evenly browned; remove with a slotted spoon and set aside. Add onion to casserole and cook a few minutes to soften. Return lamb and add all herbs, spices and garlic.

Grate lemon and orange peel; cut away pith from fruit. Divide in segments and add to casserole with grated peels, apples and honey. Pour over wine and season with salt and pepper. Cover and cook gently about 2 hours or until lamb is very tender.

Serve lamb garnished with orange and lemon slices and rosemary sprigs.

Makes 4 servings.

Note: This dish is particulary good served with a fennel and watercress salad and a dish of rice mixed with ground almonds, garlic and parsley. It is an excellent choice for a dinner party, as it can be prepared well ahead of time and seems more flavorful if left for a few hours before reheating.

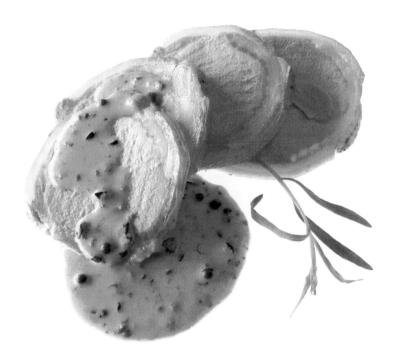

Pork with Juniper Sauce

1 (3-lb.) boneless pork loin
3 garlic cloves, slivered
Salt and pepper to taste

Sauce:
18 juniper berries, crushed
1 teaspoon green peppercorns,
  crushed
2 tablespoons brandy
2 tablespoons whipping cream
1/3 cup plain yogurt

Preheat oven to 375F (190C).
Remove skin and most of fat from pork. Make several slits in pork and insert garlic. Season pork with salt and pepper. Roll up and secure with string. Rub outside of pork with salt and pepper.
Place pork in a roasting pan and add 2 inches of water. Roast, uncovered, in oven about 1-1/2 hours or until pork is cooked. Remove from pan and set aside to cool.
To make sauce, pour off fat from pan juices. Add juniper berries, peppercorns and brandy to pan and simmer over moderate heat until reduced by half. Flame to burn off any remaining alcohol, then set aside to cool. Skim surface and whisk in cream and yogurt. Check seasoning.
Serve pork cold with juniper sauce.

Makes 6 servings.

Note: Juniper sauce is also excellent served hot with grilled or sautéed pork chops; once sauce has been flamed, stir in cream and yogurt and serve immediately.

Venison with Apples

2 (1-lb.) venison steaks
All-purpose flour
1 onion, chopped
3 strips bacon, cut in strips
2 tablespoons butter
3 apples, cored, sliced
2 green onions, chopped
4 teaspoons chopped mint

Marinade:
1/4 cup olive oil
1 onion, quartered
1 large carrot, sliced
1 stalk celery, sliced
2 garlic cloves
Bouquet garni
2 bay leaves
2 teaspoons salt
8 black peppercorns
1/3 cup red wine

To Garnish:
Shredded green onion

Lay venison steaks in a shallow dish.

To prepare marinade, in a large saucepan, heat oil. Add vegetables, garlic, herbs and seasoning and sauté until lightly browned. Add wine and let marinade bubble for 2 minutes. Pour over steaks and refrigerate 2 days.

Preheat oven to 325F (165C).

Strain marinade into a bowl; discard vegetables and herbs. Lift out steaks and dry well. Season both sides, roll up and secure with string. Dust with flour and place in an ovenproof dish. Cover with chopped onion and bacon strips; pour over marinade. Cover tightly and bake in oven 3-1/2 hours.

Remove steaks from dish and keep warm. Pour off fat from dish; strain remaining juices and reheat sauce.

Just before serving, in a skillet, melt butter. Add apple slices and sauté until golden. Sprinkle with green onions and mint.

To serve, cut steaks in thick slices and arrange on a serving dish with apple slices. Garnish with green onion and serve sauce separately.

Makes 4 servings.

Mushroom & Garlic Ragoût

3 garlic heads, separated in
  cloves, unpeeled
1 oz. dried porcini mushrooms
1 tablespoon olive oil
1 thyme sprig
1/2 cup red wine
1/2 teaspoon salt
1/2 cup beef stock
1 lb. button mushrooms
2 tablespoons whipping cream

To Garnish:
Thyme sprigs

In a small saucepan, simmer garlic cloves in water to cover 2 to 3 minutes. Drain, peel and trim root end.

In a small dish, cover porcini mushrooms with boiling water and soak 10 minutes. Drain, reserving soaking liquid.

Put garlic cloves, porcini mushrooms, oil, thyme, wine, salt, beef stock and 3 tablespoons reserved mushroom liquid in a saucepan.

Simmer, uncovered, 25 minutes.

If button mushrooms are large, cut in half. Add to saucepan, cover and cook 5 to 7 minutes, until mushrooms are cooked but still firm. Strain liquid into a small pan and reduce quickly to 2 tablespoons. Stir in 1/2 of cream. Discard thyme sprig.

Transfer mushrooms and garlic to individual serving dishes and pour over sauce. Spoon over remaining cream, garnish with thyme and serve immediately.

Makes 4 servings.

Note: If serving with roasted meat, poultry or game, 1 tablespoon meat juices can replace some of mushroom cooking liquid. Porcini mushrooms are available from Italian delicatessens; they are the same mushrooms as French *cèpes.*

Braised Endive

3 tablespoons butter
1 small onion, finely chopped
2 strips bacon, chopped
1-1/2 lbs. Belgian endive
3/4 cup chicken stock
1/2 teaspoon salt
Black pepper to taste
1 tablespoon finely chopped
  lemon balm

To Garnish:
Lemon balm sprigs

Preheat oven to 325F (165C).

In a skillet, melt butter. Sauté onion and bacon 5 minutes; remove with a slotted spoon and put into a flameproof baking dish.

Add endive to skillet and cook, turning in butter, until lightly browned on all sides. Remove with a slotted spoon and lay on top of onion and bacon. Pour over chicken stock; add salt and pepper. Cover and bake in oven 1-1/2 hours or until endive is tender. Transfer endive to a serving dish and keep warm.

Place baking dish over high heat and reduce cooking juices. Add lemon balm and pour over endive. Serve immediately, garnished with lemon balm sprigs.

Makes 4 servings.

Variations: Braising is also an excellent way of cooking celery hearts. Follow same method as above, but flavor with chopped fresh dill or parsley rather than lemon balm.

Vegetables with Ricotta

6 tomatoes
6 small zucchini
1/2 cup ricotta cheese
1/4 cup sour cream
1 teaspoon chopped lemon thyme
1 teaspoon chopped marjoram
Salt and black pepper to taste
2 tablespoons chopped green
  pitted olives
3 to 4 tablespoons chopped
  pistachio nuts
2 teaspoons dried bread crumbs
2 tablespoons olive oil

To Garnish:
Lemon thyme sprigs
Marjoram sprigs

Preheat oven to 350F (175C).
  Cut tops off tomatoes. Scoop out flesh and invert tomatoes to drain. Cut zucchini in half lengthwise and scoop out flesh.

Sieve ricotta cheese into a bowl; mix in sour cream, thyme, marjoram and season with salt and pepper.
  Fill tomatoes 3/4 full with ricotta mixture; top with chopped olives. Fill zucchini with ricotta mixture. Top with pistachio nuts, then bread crumbs.
  Place vegetables in an ovenproof dish large enough to hold them in 1 layer. Drizzle olive oil over them. Put a little water in bottom of dish and bake, uncovered, in oven 20 to 25 minutes, until zucchini are tender.
  Transfer vegetables to a serving dish and garnish with lemon thyme and marjoram sprigs. Serve hot.

Makes 6 servings.

Asparagus Gratin

1-1/2 lbs. asparagus

Sauce:
1 leek, finely chopped
2 teaspoons all-purpose flour
3/4 cup milk
4 teaspoons chopped tarragon
2 tablespoons whipping cream
Salt and black pepper to taste
1 egg

To Garnish:
Tarragon sprigs

Preheat oven to 375F (190C).

Trim and cook asparagus in usual way; drain off cooking water, reserving 1/3 cup. Set asparagus aside.

To prepare sauce, in a saucepan, melt 1/2 of butter. Add leek, cover and cook gently 5 minutes. Stir in flour and cook gently 2 to 3 minutes.

In a separate pan, heat milk and reserved asparagus cooking liquid; do not allow to boil. Add to roux and stir over low heat until sauce has thickened. Remove from heat and stir in tarragon, cream and season with salt and pepper. Beat egg lightly and stir into sauce.

Lay asparagus in a gratin dish, tips facing alternate ends. Pour over sauce, dot with remaining butter and bake in oven 10 to 12 minutes, until golden and sauce is bubbling.

Serve from baking dish, garnished with tarragon sprigs.

Makes 4 to 6 servings.

Fragrant Pilaf

3 tablespoons honey
2-1/2 cups boiling water
3 cups basmati rice
2 teaspoons salt
1/2 teaspoon ground cinnamon
6 tablespoons butter
3/4 cup blanched almonds
1 teaspooon pink peppercorns
3/4 cup chopped dried apricots
1/2 cup currants
1 tablespoon rose water

To Garnish:
Cilantro sprigs

In a bowl, place honey and boiling water; stir until dissolved. Pour into a large saucepan. Add rice, salt, cinnamon and 2/3 of butter. Bring to a rapid boil. Boil 3 minutes, then cover tightly and simmer over low heat 30 minutes.

Meanwhile, in a skillet, melt remaining butter. Add almonds and fry until lightly toasted. Add peppercorns, apricots and currants; fry 5 minutes, stirring frequently.

Add almond mixture to rice, burying it. Cover tightly and simmer over low heat 15 to 20 minutes or until all liquid is absorbed and grains of rice are separated and tender but firm. Add rose water. Let stand before serving, garnished with cilantro sprigs.

Makes 4 to 6 servings.

Note: This pilaf is excellent served with grilled kebabs and a bowl of creamy yogurt.

Variation: Use orange flower water in place of rose water.

Potatoes & Rosemary

2 lbs. potatoes
1/4 cup butter
2 onions, thinly sliced
1 (1-3/4-oz.) can anchovy fillets,
   drained, chopped
2 garlic cloves, crushed
About 5 teaspoons finely chopped
   rosemary
Salt and black pepper to taste
1 cup milk

To Garnish:
Rosemary sprigs

Slice potatoes thinly and place in a bowl of cold water until ready to use. Preheat oven to 400F (205C).

In a skillet, melt 1/2 of butter. Fry onions a few minutes until softened; set aside.

Butter a gratin dish. Drain potato slices and dry on paper towels. Place a layer of sliced potatoes in dish; cover with onions. Sprinkle on some anchovies, garlic and rosemary. Season with salt and pepper and dot with part of remaining butter. Repeat until all potatoes and onions are used, finishing with a layer of potatoes.

Pour over milk and dot with remaining butter. Bake in oven about 40 minutes or until potatoes are cooked. Check occasionally and if browning too quickly, cover with foil

Serve straight from dish, garnished with rosemary sprigs.

Makes 5 to 6 servings.

Note: These potatoes make a good accompaniment to grilled meats or they can be served for lunch with crusty bread and a crisp green salad.

Lentil & Hazelnut Salad

2 cups small green lentils
2 carrots
1 small onion
5 garlic cloves
1 bay leaf
5 to 6 parsley sprigs
3 thyme sprigs
2-1/2 cups chicken stock
2 ozs. radishes, sliced
1 cup hazelnuts, sliced
4 ozs. mozzarella cheese, cubed
4 green onions, finely chopped
4 teaspoons finely chopped
  savory

Dressing:
3/4 cup hazelnut oil
1/3 cup white wine vinegar
Salt and black pepper to taste

To Garnish:
Thyme sprigs

Put lentils, carrots, onion and 4 garlic cloves in a large saucepan. Tie bay leaf, parsley and thyme in muslin and add to pan. Add chicken stock, cover and cook 15 to 20 minutes or until lentils are tender. Discard vegetables and herbs. Drain lentils thoroughly and put into a salad bowl.

To prepare dressing, crush remaining garlic clove. In a small bowl, blend together crushed garlic, oil and vinegar until creamy. Pour over lentils. Season with salt and pepper, cover and chill at least 30 minutes.

Just before serving, add radishes, hazelnuts, mozzarella cheese, green onions and savory to salad and toss well. Check seasoning. Garnish with thyme sprigs to serve.

Makes 6 servings.

Jerusalem Artichoke Salad

2 lbs. Jerusalem artichokes
1 teaspoon salt
3 strips bacon
1 small French bread baguette,
    cut in small cubes
2 to 3 tablespoons snipped chives

Dressing:
1/3 cup olive oil
Juice 1/2 lemon
1/2 teaspoon salt
Black pepper to taste

To Garnish:
Lemon slices
Few chives

Cook artichokes in boiling salted water until tender but firm.

Meanwhile, prepare dressing. In a small bowl, blend together oil, lemon juice and salt. Season with pepper.

Drain artichokes. Cool slightly, then peel and cut in slices. Put into a salad bowl and mix with dressing. Set aside to cool.

In a skillet, fry bacon in its own fat until crisp. Remove with a slotted spoon and drain on paper towels, then chop. Reserve bacon fat in pan.

Use bread cubes to prepare croûtons. Fry in bacon fat, adding a little olive oil if necessary, until crisp and golden; drain.

Just before serving, add bacon and croûtons to artichokes; toss well and sprinkle with chives. Serve immediately, garnished with lemon slices trimmed with chives.

Makes 4 servings.

Note: Jerusalem artichokes are also excellent boiled, then pureed and flavored with chervil. Serve as an accompaniment to grilled and roasted meats.

Hot Summer Salad

1 yellow bell pepper
1 red bell pepper
1 green bell pepper
1 small fresh or canned hot chili
   pepper
1/3 cup olive oil
Juice 2 limes
1 garlic clove
Salt and black pepper to taste
1 large avocado
8 ozs. green beans, blanched,
   trimmed
2 tomatoes, sliced
4 green onions, chopped
2 tablespoons finely chopped
   parsley

Place bell peppers under a hot grill until skin is blistered and charred, turning occasionally. Cook, then peel off blackened skin.

Slit bell peppers open and remove core and seeds. Cut flesh in long thin strips and place in a bowl.

If using fresh chili, remove seeds and finely chop; if using canned chili, rinse well before chopping. Add to bowl.

In a blender or food processor fitted with a metal blade, process oil, lime juice and garlic until smooth and creamy. Pour over bell peppers. Season with salt and pepper and chill until required.

Just before serving, slice avocado and add to bell peppers with green beans, tomatoes and green onions. Toss gently. Check seasoning and sprinkle with parsley.

Makes 6 servings.

Note Omit chili pepper if a milder flavor is preferred.

Chicken & Dandelion Salad

1 (2-1/2-lb.) smoked chicken
40 dandelion leaves
4 stalks celery, cut in strips
1/2 cucumber, cut in strips
2 tablespoons olive oil
2 shallots, chopped
2 tablespoons chopped mint
1 tablespoon raisins
2 tablespoon pine nuts
1 garlic clove, crushed
2 teaspoons red wine vinegar
Salt and black pepper to taste
2 tablespoons crème fraîche

Skin chicken and cut flesh in serving pieces.

In a large saucepan of boiling salted water, plunge dandelion leaves 20 seconds to blanch. Drain and refresh with cold water. Drain and dry leaves carefully with paper towels.

In a large salad bowl, arrange chicken, dandelion leaves, celery and cucumber.

Heat oil in a skillet. Add shallots and sauté until softened. Add mint, raisins, pine nuts and garlic. Sauté gently 5 minutes more, taking care that garlic does not burn. Cool, then stir in vinegar.

Season dressing with salt and pepper. Add crème fraîche and pour dressing over chicken salad. Serve immediately.

Makes 4 servings.

Rhubarb & Ginger Ice Cream

1 lb. rhubarb, cut in small pieces
1/3 cup superfine sugar
4 egg yolks
1-1/4 cups whipping cream
1 (2-inch) piece stem ginger in
    syrup, finely chopped
2 tablespoons ginger syrup

To Decorate:
Mint sprigs

To Serve:
Langues de chats or ladyfinger
    cookies

Put rhubarb and sugar in top half of a double boiler or a bowl set over a saucepan of simmering water. Cover and cook over low heat until tender. Puree in a blender or food processor or rub through a sieve; cool.

Place egg yolks and cream in top half of double boiler or bowl as before and whisk over low heat until thickened. Remove from heat immediately and continue whisking a few minutes; cool.

Stir rhubarb mixture into custard. Add ginger and ginger syrup; taste for sweetness—add a little more syrup if necessary. Pour mixture into container of an electric sorbetière and freeze according to manufacturer's instructions. Or pour into a freezer-proof container, cover and freeze about 3 hours, until firm. Stir several times during freezing to avoid ice crystals forming.

Scoop ice cream into chilled glass dishes and decorate with mint sprigs. Serve with langues de chats or ladyfinger cookies.

Makes 6 to 8 servings.

Variation: Use gooseberries instead of rhubarb.

Lavender Ice Cream

1/2 oz. lavender flowers
1-1/4 cups whipping cream
4 egg yolks
1/3 cup superfine sugar
1 to 2 drops blue food coloring

Sauce:
3 ripe persimmons
5 teaspoons white wine

To Decorate:
Mint or lemon balm sprigs

Put lavender flowers and cream in a saucepan and heat gently 15 minutes. Turn off heat and leave to infuse 20 minutes.

Strain cream into top part of a double boiler or a bowl set over a saucepan of simmering water, pressing to extract oil from flowers. Add egg yolks and sugar; whisk over low heat until mixture has thickened. Remove from heat. Add blue food coloring and continue whisking for a few minutes; cool.

Pour mixture into container of an electric sorbetière and freeze according to manufacturer's instructions. Or pour into a freezer-proof container, cover and freeze about 3 hours, until firm. Stir occasionally during freezing to avoid ice crystals forming.

Meanwhile, to prepare sauce, halve persimmons and scoop out flesh. Place in a blender or food processor with wine and puree until smooth.

Scoop ice cream into chilled dishes. Decorate with mint or lemon balm sprigs and serve with persimmon sauce.

Makes 6 servings.

Variation: Serve lavender ice cream with raspberry rather than persimmon sauce. To prepare sauce, puree 12 ounces fresh raspberries in a blender or food processor. Sieve to remove seeds, then sweeten to taste with sugar.

Almond Rose Meringue

6 egg whites
1-1/4 cups ground almonds
1 cup superfine sugar
3/4 cup all-purpose flour
Few drops rose water concentrate

Rose Cream:
3 egg yolks
1/2 cup powdered sugar
2 teaspoons rose water
  concentrate
18 tablespoons unsalted butter,
  softened
Few drops of red food coloring,
  if desired

Crystallized Rose Petals:
3 to 4 roses
1 egg white, beaten
Superfine sugar for coating

To Decorate:
Powered sugar

Preheat oven to 350F (175C).
  Whisk egg whites until stiff and dry. Add ground almonds, sugar, flour and rose water concentrate; mix well.
  Butter 4 baking sheets generously. This is important, otherwise meringues will stick—use about 1/4 cup melted butter. Mark a 12-inch circle on each baking sheet and cover with meringue mixture, spreading it thinly and evenly. Bake in oven about 30 minutes, until golden. Trim neatly and place on wire racks to cool; keep meringues flat.
  To crystallize rose petals, dip petals into beaten egg white, then into sugar. Place on wire rack to dry.
  To make Rose Cream, place all ingredients in a blender or food processor and blend until smooth.
  To assemble, place 1 meringue on a platter and cover with 1/3 of Rose Cream. Repeat layers, finishing with a meringue. Dust top with powdered sugar and decorate with crystallized rose petals.

Makes 8 servings.

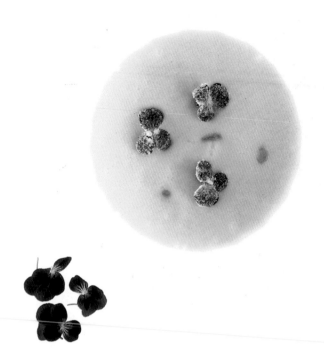

Mascarpone with Violets

12 ladyfinger cookies
1 lb. mascarpone cheese
4 egg yolks
2 tablespoons Armagnac
1/3 cup superfine sugar
1/4 cup chopped candied angelica

Crystallized Violets:
1 bunch of violets
1 egg white, beaten
Superfine sugar

Line bottom of a serving dish with ladyfinger cookies, trimming to fit if necessary.

Sieve mascarpone into a bowl. Mix in egg yolks, Armagnac and sugar and blend well.

Set aside 2 to 3 teaspoons chopped angelica for decorations; stir remaining into mascarpone. Pour over cookies. Chill 2 to 3 hours.

To crystallize violets, hold by stem, dip into beaten egg white, then into sugar. Set on wire rack to dry.

Decorate dessert with reserved angelica and crystallized violets to serve.

Makes 6 servings.

Note: Mascarpone is a very rich smooth cream cheese, available from Italian delicatessens and some supermarkets. It is used primarily in desserts. For a less rich dessert with a grainy texture, use ricotta cheese.

Spiced Plums in Rum

1-1/3 cups dark rum
1 small cinnamon stick
1/2 vanilla bean
3 cloves
1/4 cup superfine sugar
12 dark plums

Sabayon Sauce:
3 egg yolks
3 tablespoons superfine sugar
2 tablespoons whipping cream

To Decorate:
Mint sprigs

Place rum, spices and sugar in a small saucepan and simmer over low heat 20 minutes. Flame to burn off any remaining alcohol.

Puncture plum skins 6 or 7 times with a sharp skewer or needle. Place in a bowl and pour over rum syrup. Chill at least 24 hours.

An hour before serving, remove bowl from refrigerator and let stand at room temperature. Pour off rum syrup and set aside; discard spices.

To make Sabayon Sauce, put egg yolks, sugar, cream and 1/4 cup of rum syrup in top part of a double boiler or a bowl set over a saucepan of simmering water. Whisk until light and frothy.

To serve, place 3 plums on each plate and spoon over Sabayon Sauce. Decorate with mint sprigs.

Makes 4 servings.

Note: These plums can be kept covered in the refrigerator for several months. They are equally delicious served plain with a little rum syrup as a sauce or with fresh whipping cream. Or they can be pitted, pureed and used to flavor homemade ice cream.

Cinnamon Soufflé

3/4 cup whipping cream
3/4 cup half and half
1/4 (8-oz.) pkg. cream cheese,
 softened (2 ozs.)
1 (3-inch) cinnamon stick
6 tablespoons butter
1/3 cup all-purpose flour
2 teaspoons ground cinnamon
4 eggs, separated
1/4 cup superfine sugar
Pinch of salt

Orange Sauce:
3 oranges
2 tablespoons Grand Marnier
2 teaspoons superfine sugar
1/4 cup half and half

Blend cream, half and half and cream cheese together. Put in top of a double boiler or a bowl set over a saucepan of gently simmering water. Add cinnamon stick and heat gently 2 hours.

In a saucepan, melt butter. Stir in flour and cook a few minutes to make a roux; remove from heat.

Discard cinnamon stick and pour warm cream mixture into roux, stirring constantly. Add ground cinnamon and simmer 30 minutes stirring occasionally. Remove from heat.

Meanwhile, preheat oven to 400F (205C). Butter a 2-quart soufflé dish.

Beat egg yolks and sugar together and add to cream mixture. Whisk egg whites with salt until very stiff; fold into cream mixture. Pour into prepared dish and bake in oven 25 to 30 minutes.

Meanwhile, prepare sauce. Grate rind of 1 orange; squeeze juice of 3 oranges. Put in a small saucepan with Grand Marnier and sugar. Boil until reduced by half. Just before serving, stir in half and half.

Serve soufflé immediately with sauce served separately.

Makes 6 servings.

Fresh Raspberry Tart

Pastry:
1-3/4 cups all-purpose flour
Pinch salt
3/4 cup butter
2 tablespoons superfine sugar
About 1/3 cup chilled water

Filling:
1 lb. raspberries
1/3 cup superfine sugar
1-1/2 teaspoons ground cinnamon

Marzipan:
3/4 cup ground almonds
1/4 cup powdered sugar, sifted
1 small egg, beaten

To Decorate:
2 to 3 elderflowers, if desired

To Serve:
Whipping cream

To prepare pastry, sift flour and salt into a large bowl. Cut in butter, then stir in sugar. Add chilled water and mix to a firm dough. Wrap in plastic wrap and chill about 30 minutes.

To prepare filling, place raspberries in a bowl, sprinkle with sugar and cinnamon and let stand 1 hour.

To prepare marzipan, mix together ground almonds and powdered sugar. Add egg to mixture, working it in with your hands. Knead until marzipan is smooth.

Preheat oven to 400F (205C). On a lightly floured surface, roll out pastry thinly and line a 10-inch flan dish. Prick bottom of pastry and fill with dried beans. Bake blind 8 to 10 minutes or until firm and golden; cool.

Just before serving, roll out marzipan and trim to a circle to fit bottom of pastry. Place in pastry, then spoon raspberries with their juice on top.

Serve immediately, decorated with elderflowers, if desired, and accompanied by whipped cream.

Makes 6 servings.

Lemon & Cardamom Cake

**About 3 teaspoons shelled
  cardamom seeds**
2 lemons
1 cup ground almonds
1/2 cup dried bread crumbs
1/3 cup superfine sugar
4 eggs, separated
Pinch salt

To Serve:
Whipping cream, if desired
Shredded lemon peel, if desired

Preheat oven to 375F (190C). Butter a 6-1/2-inch springform pan.

Grind cardamom seeds in a mortar. Grate lemon peel and squeeze juice from lemons.

In a bowl, mix together ground almonds, 2 teaspoons of ground cardamom, bread crumbs and lemon peel and juice. Mix in sugar.

Beat egg yolks and add to almond mixture. Whisk egg whites with salt until stiff; carefully fold into mixture. Pour into prepared pan.

Bake in oven about 40 minutes or until a skewer inserted into center of cake comes out clean. Cool in pan.

Serve topped with piped whipped cream and shredded lemon peel, if desired.

Makes 6 servings.

Variation: Instead of lemons, this cake can be flavored with oranges. Substitute lemon juice and peel with orange juice and peel. Sprinkle with a few drops of orange flower water before serving.

Grapefruit Ratafia

3 large grapefruit
1/2 cup coriander seeds
1 cup superfine sugar
3 (2-inch) cinnamon sticks
3 cups brandy

Pare peel from grapefruit and cut in strips; set aside. Squeeze grapefruit juice and set aside.

Crack coriander seeds in a pestle and mortar.

Put sugar, grapefruit peel and juice, cracked coriander seeds and cinnamon sticks into a 2-quart bottle or crock. Add brandy and cover tightly. Store in a cool dark place 2 months.

Strain liqueur through fine muslin into bottles and cork. Store in a cool dark place.

Makes about 1 quart.

Note: Ratafias are often drunk as a liqueur and would be served after a meal, but they are also a refreshing and unusual apéritif.

Variations: Ratafias can be made with other flavorings such as anise, juniper berries and fennel; with other fruit, such as black currants and oranges, and with peach and apricot pits.

Ginger Champagne Punch

4 (750-ml.) bottles champagne or
   dry sparkling white wine
Few handfuls borage flowers
2 teaspoons ground ginger
1/2 cup superfine sugar
1-1/4 cups water
Juice 1 lemon
40 ozs. pineapple juice
40 ozs. ginger ale

Pour 1 bottle of champagne or sparkling wine into ice-cube trays; put a borage flower into each cube and freeze. Place a large punch bowl in the freezer to chill.

To prepare syrup, put ginger, sugar and water in a saucepan. Heat gently to a low simmer; simmer gently 5 minutes. Remove from heat and cool.

Just before serving, take punch bowl from freezer and pour in syrup and lemon and pineapple juices. Stir, then add ginger ale and remaining champagne.

Decorate each glass with a borage flower ice cube before serving.

Makes about 4-1/2 quarts.

Variation: For a more alcholic punch, replace ginger syrup with ginger wine.

Instead of freezing borage flowers in ice cubes, float them on top of punch.

— INDEX —